GOOGLE CLASSROOM

The 2020 Complete Guide for Students and Teachers on How to Benefit from Distance Learning and Setup Your Virtual Classroom

By

© Anna Smith

PUBLISHED BY: © Anna Smith

ISBN:

TABLE OF CONTENTS

INTRODUCTION 1

CHAPTER 1: WHAT IS GOOGLE CLASSROOM? 3

Google Classroom: The School In The Time Of The Coronavirus 3

How to set up Google Classroom in three steps 11

Benefits of Google Classroom for Teachers 13

The advantages of Google Classroom in the course of classes . 15

Benefits Of Google Classroom For Students 16

CHAPTER 2 : ACTIVE LEARNING AND HOME SCHOOLING 18

Classroom interaction: How does Google Classroom help? 18

Elements Involved In Online Teaching And Learning 22

Google Classroom: the class goes digital 37

CHAPTER 3: GOOGLE CLASSROOM AND HOME SCHOOLING 40

Is online learning as effective as face-to-face learning? 40

Virtual education: Advantages, myths and tips to improve results 46

CHAPTER 4: TEACHER VIEW 52

GOOGLE CLASSROOM FOR TEACHERS 52

Creating And Setting Classes 53
Inviting your students on Google Classroom 54
How to create and collect assignments from students 56
How To Use Question 60
How to Use Rubrics 65
CHAPTER 5: STUDENT VIEW 69
Google Classroom For Students: Accessing Google Classroom 69
Basic Guide To Google Classroom For Students 75
CHAPTER 6: EXTENSION AND APPS 83
The 13 Best Must-Have Google Chrome Extensions for Teachers 83
The 12 Best Google Classroom Apps 91
CHAPTER 7: OTHER AMAZING THINGS ABOUT GOOGLE CLASSROOM 96
Ten Reasons Why You Should Use Google Classroom 96
50 Things You Can Do With Google Classroom 100
Advantages And Limitations Of Google Classroom 102
CHAPTER 8: GOOGLE CLASSROOM TIPS AND TRICKS 106
3 Tips to Organize Your Google Classroom - 106
CONCLUSION 113
APPRECIATION 115

INTRODUCTION

An increasing number of teachers are using the Google Classroom platform, which allows you to focus less on technology and more on teaching , as it allows you to organize a virtual classroom and distance lessons without necessarily being a technology professional.

In this book, we will see all you need to get started with Google Classroom and what it allows you to do. Next, we will see how to set up a class and create jobs such as assignments, quiz assignments, questions and provide teaching materials. Let's jump right in.

CHAPTER 1: WHAT IS GOOGLE CLASSROOM?

Google Classroom: The School In The Time Of The Coronavirus

Google's distance learning program has become one of the most widely used and interesting globally.

Coronavirus changed the lives of many of us but most of all it changed the lives of children and young people. In fact, for two months now, schools have been closed, the rules have changed and teaching, with all the necessary difficulties, has moved to the homes of children and teachers , filtered by computer screens and the speed of internet connections.

A not entirely new way of learning and teaching but unexpectedly becoming central in recent times. The tool of the moment could therefore only be **Google Classroom**, the suite of programs and services designed by Mountain View to unite teachers and students. Does the program replace classroom lessons worthily?

What it is

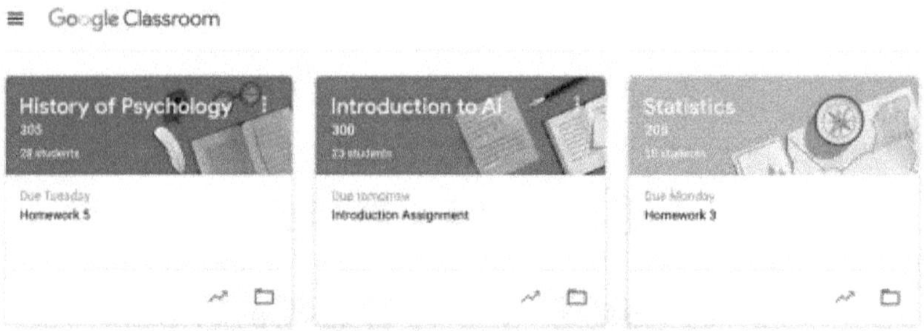

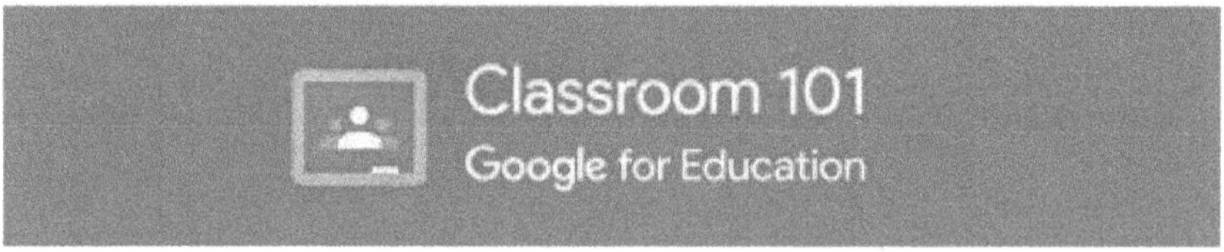

In general, Google Classroom is nothing more than a program that facilitates distance learning by offering a series of sharing possibilities and total synergy with the classic functions of the Google world. Available for free for six years and already widely used by many teachers, **the program has become the most used by teachers in these times of pandemic .** Its functions allow you to assign exercises, tests and questionnaires, store didactic material in a shared space, share videos and exchange messages quickly and quickly.

A unique code is enough for the pupils of their class to create a "private environment" quite similar to that of the school walls, accessible only to the teacher who created the room and to the pupils to whom the code was sent.

With a Google account in a few minutes of configuration you can take advantage of the service, accessible from a PC or smartphone via an application. Inside, students can check the deadlines of tasks and checks, be updated when new content arrives, receive grades. Maximum also the possibility of communication, both between pupils and with the teacher, inevitable the possibility of making video lessons.

Six years of history

Announced and previewed for selected users on May 6, 2014, Google Classroom was initially designed for members of the **G Suite for Education program** . Initially, even after the official release, the app was linked to paid G Suite members. A strategy that lasted more or less three years: in March 2017, the service was open to any user with a Google account, also giving non-G Suite members the opportunity to participate in lessons or create new ones.

A major update of the program was launched in 2018, with new work sections, improved assessment interface and new features for students and teachers. Today Classroom, in addition to its 78 illustrated themes, offers full compatibility with **Google Drive** for archiving and sending documents, with **Gmail** for communications, with **Calendar** for managing deadlines and notices and with various management and file creation programs such as **Google Docs, Sheets and Presentations .**

More recently came the total compatibility with **Hangout** to manage a more immediate communication between the components of a class and to give life to real video lesson sessions.

Facilitated entry

The diffusion of Classroom was certainly helped by the undeniable ease of use of its services and by their degree of familiarity with users' habits. Having a Google account means knowing already many of the services at the basis of the functioning of your school program: the strong point of the app is in fact its **very strong synergy with the Google galaxy** , perfectly integrated within it. Drive is used to store documents and lessons, Hangouts for video lessons or chats, all without having to pay absolutely anything, with maximum compatibility with many apps and without any type of advertising.

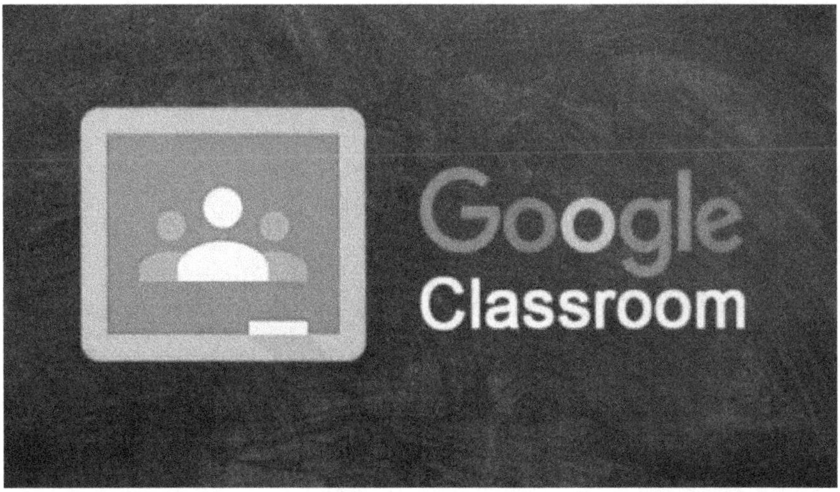

A differentiated service, different in the setting between teachers and students, but which shares the same work tools with maximum compatibility. Basically it is enough to have a minimum of familiarity with the various programs of the Google suite to be able to use everything with maximum effectiveness. A simplicity of purpose that had brought Classroom to the center of the scene even in unsuspected times and that has now made it essential to carry on the educational work in lockdown times .

Teachers, students and parents

The teachers represent the nerve center of Classroom : from their page they can manage the various classes they have created, with the possibility of sharing materials, assigning tasks and checking the progress of each work assigned to their students. Through the calendar you can manage appointments or deadlines and organize group meetings. **The students** , for their part, in addition to participating in collective activities, have numerous possibilities to complete the tasks assigned to them. These can be managed quickly and intuitively, with the possibility of choosing which app to use to complete the work according to the request of your teacher.

Once completed, everything can be uploaded and will be viewed by the teacher, who will have full control of all the papers and the relative deadlines. Also interesting is the **possibility for parents to monitor** their children's **class** through the function, always filtered by teachers, to have access to an email system in which to be updated on the progress of the work, the lessons held and more general information. on the progress of the class. In short, a school microcosm in all respects.

The evaluation system

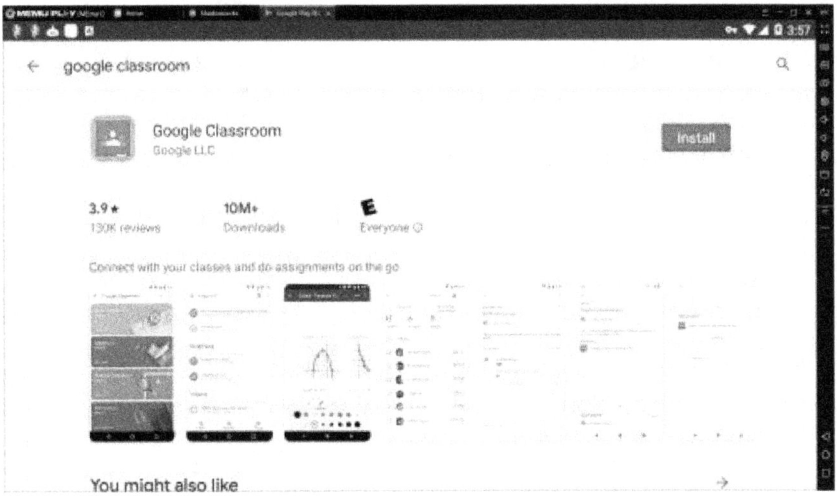

One of the most appreciated functions of Classroom is certainly that of evaluations, with **the possibility for teachers to provide feedback on the work done by students** . The voting schemes are numerous, with options to attach files to the assignments, possibility to monitor the progress of each student, also making comments, changes or annotations in real time. Once their work has been completed and sent, teachers have the possibility of returning them with notes and corrections which in turn allow the pupils themselves to correct where they have done wrong.

A real-time evaluation and correction system that allows you to follow step by step the processing of everything you want, correcting errors in the bud and with the possibility of interaction during the performance of activities that are difficult to replicate in normal conditions or with traditional methods . A possibility of no small importance and certainly a positive aspect in an emergency situation like this and which, if exploited properly, **could make Classroom a very useful tool also alongside the more traditional teaching .**

A school for everyone, even from a distance

Over the years, however, many criticisms have been made towards Classroom, starting with a lack of openness to services or files external to the tools provided by Google and to a limited number of verification tools such as quizzes or automatic tests. There have also been accusations in the not exactly transparent management of user data, which is very valuable since it is almost always a question of minors or children.

Google has always reiterated its attention to privacy but the **storage and archiving of student data remains one of the hottest topics that revolve around the program**. Despite this, the great utility of the service for students and teachers is undeniable; it is essential, in fact, that teaching continues at all costs and that education does not stop even in conditions like these.

All programs that help distance learning are therefore fundamental, even more so if integrated with applications that many of us already use every day such as those of Google. It will be essential that these tools become more and more commonly used even in normal conditions, because they are useful for improving a teaching and school too often anchored to the past. At the same time, it will be **essential to protect all parties involved and ensure that these instruments do not become discriminators or amplifiers of differences .**

Not everyone, in fact, has the possibility to access certain tools or to fast connections that allow you to use them and not everyone is able to better understand all the functions. Giving equal access and use to everyone will be essential for an online teaching model to work and be sustainable in the future. Having the best of tools in your hands is useless if it cannot be used to the best of all sides. And this, in a delicate world like that of education and school, we must never forget it.

How to set up Google Classroom in three steps

1. **Sign in** with your school account or a regular gmail. When you go to **classroom.google.com** you can use Classroom by logging in using a G suite email address or you can use a normal gmail account.

2. **Create your first lesson .** Click the "+" button in the upper right corner. Choose "create course". Here, enter some detailed information about your class. The class name will be the class title so you can find it in seconds. Then click "create".

3. **Invite students to your class .** Once you have created the course you will see under the title the code to be

used to invite your students. Go to the People menu and from there start inviting your students by entering a name or email address.

Now your online course is ready! At least, it's there and everyone can access it. There are a few other things you need to do before you can take off seriously.

Create and assign a job to your course

To **create assignments to assign to your class** in the upper menu, go to "Course work" and click on "+ Create", a drop-down window will open which will propose the possible jobs you can create.

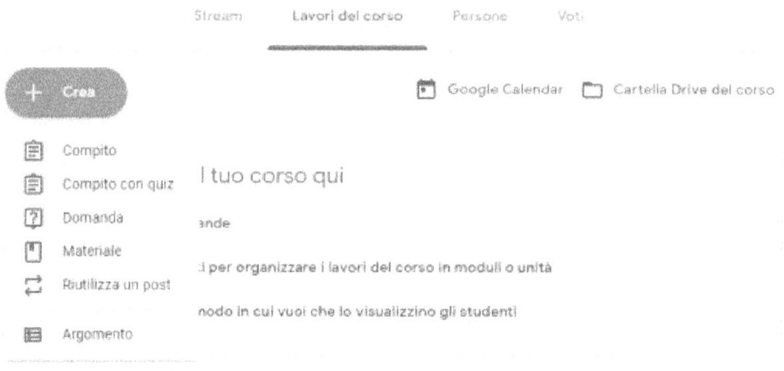

For example, choosing "Task with Quiz" will open a panel where you can configure the work to be assigned, you will only have to enter the Title, if you want the instructions and click on "Blank Quiz" in which to enter the questions, multiple answers and wanting the score.

If you want to **add material to share, all** you have to do is click on "+ Create" and select "Material", assign a title and description and add a file in Google Drive, a link, a file on your computer or a video Youtube

Of course, there is much more to say about Google Classroom, what we have just faced is the basic path that will still allow you to create a class and assign tasks to students.

Benefits of Google Classroom for Teachers

The new Google platform is designed to improve the relationship between students and teachers. Google Classroom facilitates interaction in classes.

Google has launched its new platform to improve interaction with students in class

- Sharing documents with your students and notifying them of the exam call can be done immediately thanks to the new Google platform.
- Students can now deliver their work in digital format online thanks to Google Classroom. This platform improves teacher-student communication.
- Google Classroom helps improve interaction with students, making classes more fluid.

Google has launched its new platform to improve interaction with students in class. **Google Classroom** keeps students and teacher in contact.

The Internet makes people's lives easier in different areas. Thanks to **Google Classroom** it is easier to follow the classes and share the material with the students. This online platform is designed to improve communication and work flow between student and teacher.

Access to Google Classroom only requires a Google account and an **internet connection**. The platform works as a social network designed to facilitate the topics discussed in class.

Getting the necessary material to **follow the classes** to the students is usually difficult for the teachers. Google Classroom has developed a new solution . This platform allows you to share documents and create a calendar where students can find out the dates of the exams and the delivery of assignments.

The classroom is **a space for coexistence .** The Internet allows this space to be extended after school hours. The platform designed by Google allows students to access all the information of the class online, so they can review the subject and catch up, in the event that they have been ill and have not gone to class.

The advantages of Google Classroom in the course of classes

1. Share the exam schedule and work assignments with the students

Google Classroom allows you to share relevant information about the course of the subject with students. This way they can easily find out when there is an exam or when they have to submit a job.

2. Facilitate the delivery of class work in digital format

The delivery of works thanks to Google Classroom can be done online. This way you don't have to print your jobs and do this paper waste. This application facilitates the digital delivery of class work.

3. Sending extra material to prepare the classes

Many teachers ask their students to do readings before classes begin. The Google platform allows these texts to be shared with students in a quick and comfortable way.

4. Inform the student of news when they cannot go to the classroom

To update a student who has not been able to attend class, Google Classroom is perfect. The sick student can be in contact with the teacher's classes through the internet.

Benefits Of Google Classroom For Students

Responsive

Google Classroom can be run on all devices without any problem, be it a Phone or Android, Tablet or PC.

Promote communication and collaborative work

Being a product of google, This platform is **integrated with Google Doc**, so it **allows the creation of documents, tables and presentations jointly among students,** this can be a tool to promote group work and the use of digital tools.

Leaving homework and assignments becomes easier

Thanks to Google Clasrroom, leaving a task or subject can be simplified to 1 click, so you can send the time to print material, distribute it, and then collect and classify it, this is a great relief for both the teacher and the students.

Goodbye to the papers

Caring for the environment is a topic that is becoming increasingly relevant, just one of the main objectives of this platform is to save paper, avoid printing readings, formats and educational material, and share it all with one click.

Friendly use

Google Classroom is very easy to use, so you don't need to spend hours learning how to use this platform, it only takes about 15 min to understand how the most basic features work.

Has an integration with the Google Suite

Being a Google product, Classroom is integrated with the entire google suite so you can share information from the following applications

- Google DRIVE
- Google Calendar
- Google Sheets
- Youtube
- Google Forms

CHAPTER 2 :
ACTIVE LEARNING AND HOME SCHOOLING

Classroom interaction: How does Google Classroom help?

There is a notable change in educational practices, mainly to increasingly integrate technology in a way that is beneficial to teachers and students . Google Classroom, an application that is part of Google for Education, is one of those tools that helps to streamline the learning process.

Known for often facilitating communication between the class, the application has many other functions that deserve to be explored. And, contrary to popular belief, it is also very useful in classroom courses and not only in distance learning.

New to Classroom yet? Are you wondering how it can make your graduation much more interactive and profitable? So keep reading this post to take these and other questions!

What is Google Classroom

In 2014, Google For Education arrived in Brazil promising to bring a whole new perspective on the integration between technology and education. The well-known multinational's proposal is to offer resources to institutions, teachers and students to streamline the teaching-learning process and update educational practices.

G Suite For Education, for example, is available for free and integrates access to institutional email, unlimited storage on Google Drive, Calendar, Google Sheets, Forms and Slides. Another important Google For Education tool is Google Classroom, an online classroom mirror that provides more exchange between students and faculty.

This application is a clear example that technology does not separate, but rather when it is well used.

Google Classroom is a management, organization and collaboration tool that makes learning much more productive. Through the platform it is possible to send papers, receive grades, answer questions with teachers and fellow students and much more.

The application's practical interface allows even those who are not very familiar with other technological resources to use it without difficulty. The goal is to make the dynamics of the classes more attractive and, at the same time, more accessible.

Digital classroom in practice

But how does it all work, in practical terms? Each student at the institution must register using a specific institutional email for this purpose, which is made available by the institution. Afterwards, the teacher is responsible for connecting all of his students in an online class through the Classroom.

From there, the infinite possibilities of the application will be available, which can and should be used. For the teacher, the tool helps in the management of classes and in the ease in dealing with administrative issues, checking grades, passing on announcements and inserting evaluations in the system.

Students also benefit from the tool, making it possible to send jobs and activities much more easily. But the interaction provided by Classroom goes far beyond that and can "save" the undergraduate experience for students.

The lack of updating of teaching methods and individualized monitoring of students are considered two of the main reasons that lead to school dropout in higher education. According to research published in 2007 by the Journal of College Student Retention , innovations in the teaching process and greater communication between teachers and students are fundamental stimuli that lead to the conclusion of the course.

This, in fact, is the main proposal of the tool. Can be used at any time, it promotes instant communication and serves almost as an educational social network.

Class members can post links, comments and ask questions, having the opportunity to project their voice without the limited time and space, which happens in a conventional classroom.

Teachers can also monitor each student's progress in activities, checking where they need the most support and intervention. There is still space for the assessment to be made in detail, as the digital medium guarantees this flexibility.

Online and offline

In the case of a distance learning college, constant communication and interaction are fundamental and even define the quality of the course offered. As distance education courses do not have the presence factor, they need to abuse all available technology to stimulate learning.

The Classroom guarantees fluidity in logistics and a feeling of closeness to the teacher, important requirements so that the student does not feel that he is alone in this journey.

For a face-to-face graduation, the new dynamic makes classes more stimulating, encourages the participation of all students and still allows for a much more active learning process.

There is still the possibility to connect Classroom with other applications and enhance its functionality. Tools like Classcraft and Quizizz turn regular activities into missions or quizzes, making any job much more fun, without losing focus or quality.

Continue our section on Google tools for a simple dynamic and inclusive teaching.

Google offers free tools that are useful for both teachers and students.

No more long training courses for external management that need constant updates and are difficult to use or superfluous in everyday life.

Elements Involved In Online Teaching And Learning

Teaching and learning

Teaching and learning from virtuality today requires teachers capable of transforming their pedagogical practice using new information and communication technologies (ICT) to serve their students and face the cultural and technical challenges that lead to dynamic and complex change in what to teach, how to teach and why to teach. These conditions promote a personalized and collaborative learning process and a teaching action that seeks to satisfy the needs and interests of students for the development of their abilities through interaction with the virtual context. In this sense, the purpose of this essay is to reflect on the process of teaching and learning from virtuality considering the educational theoretical elements involved in this process. For it, virtual education and its elements, collaborative learning, virtual teaching strategies and teacher competencies in this educational modality were addressed.

Teachers in their practice are expected to promote a transformative pedagogical education that can awaken in the group of students the motivation to learn actively and according to the advances that society presents.

Introduction

Currently, the world is facing a series of historical changes of a political, social, economic and technological nature, which, if you know how to cope, you can make the best of them for the well-being and progress of the peoples; however, this requires time to analyze, understand and deal with them. Education as a factor of social development has not escaped these processes, so, according to Tedesco (2009), it is necessary for education to evolve and transform so that nations can assimilate these changes and travel alongside them, and not behind.

Thus, the author in reference states that traditional education is not responding to current economic demands, so, according to Polanco (2011), this education, also called traditional face-to-face education, treats the student as a mere spectator, in the which the didactic act becomes an illusion; hence the urgency to reform it and consolidate a new educational commitment, which fosters the formation of an individual with better human, intellectual and social capacities, with an interest in experimentation, creativity, autonomy in decisions, responsibility and cooperation in the work they do. . Salinas (2004) points out that, to adapt and transform this reality of today's society, Educational institutions must become more flexible and develop ways of integration and virtual teaching that includes ICT in educational training processes. For his part, Barriga (2009) indicates that the new demands directed at the teaching profession demand that teachers be responsible for the technological literacy of their students and for mastering a diversity of skills required in the context of the demands of society. of knowledge.

In this regard, Lagos (2010) states that ICTs have become an indispensable tool for most teacher activities; They offer a variety of resources to use in classrooms and enrich the teaching-learning process. The digital world is gradually incorporated into educational institutions, but technology alone does not improve the quality of the teaching-learning process; a change in the way of teaching and learning is necessary because if not, it would fall into the same mistakes of traditional education; therefore, it is important to know the elements that allow virtual education to be carried out in a fruitful way; you cannot continue to teach future generations with the means of the past.

Virtual educational platforms are a tool that introduce the teacher to the creation of courses and workshops, simply and quickly, that allow managing and organizing content tailored to the user. As good examples and among the best known are Dokeos and Moodle, which have been developed around the educational field and give this type of training a great pedagogical interest that generates personalized education and a diversity of courses adapted to all profiles and demands. The incorporation of these platforms in the educational field should not only focus on the inclusion of educational materials, but also on the collaborative work that these environments promote, as well as the didactic skills that they can generate with their application. These spaces have different types of tools: content, communication and evaluation and monitoring. All of them are essential for students' educational and didactic learning and allow creating content adapted to defined objectives, procedures and results, as well as collaborating with other users to help us delve deeper into the concept of collective training.

Elements Of Virtual Education

Camacho (2010) states that virtual education, even if it seems contradictory, does allow personal contact between the teacher and the student: the exchange of written messages and the possibility of detailed progress monitoring provides the teacher with a knowledge of the apprentice many times greater than in classroom courses; The information can also be adapted to users due to the modularity of the content. Therefore, to operate within virtual education it is essential to know the elements to impart learning with the use of technology:

Exploration: the use of the internet or, more precisely, the World Wide Web as an exploration tool opens the doors of an inexhaustible source of information and resources to the teacher and the student.

Experience: The virtual student is involved in a new social and learning experience that may include direct communication with his teacher, discussions with his classmates or individual study of content at his own pace.

Commitment: Virtual courses offer the student a unique opportunity to share experiences with others, reinforcing the sense of collaboration and community. Furthermore, the student receives control of her time and resources and can choose the best learning path according to her preferences and abilities.

Flexibility: from anywhere, anytime, students can access their virtual courses. It is estimated that approximately 80% of companies have already solved their internet access, so the technical barriers to access for working students have already been overcome.

News: Teachers have the opportunity to update their materials and discussion topics instantly, keeping courses fresh and consistent with today. This supposes that the teacher, when using ICT as tools in the didactic act, faces cultural and technical challenges that lead to a dynamic and complex change in what to teach, how to teach and why to teach. For this reason, virtual education supports pedagogy through innovative strategies to develop the learning process by easing the great cognitive barriers and blocks that arise with traditional education.

Teaching And Learning Strategies In Virtual Education

Esteban (2009) explains that the teaching and learning strategies used in virtual education are generally classified according to cognitive activities. In accordance with this criterion, they are classified from the most basic operations to the most elaborate in associative, elaboration, organization and support. Associative ones are the simplest and involve basic operations that do not in themselves promote relations between knowledge, but can be the basis for its subsequent elaboration, since they increase the probability of literally remembering the information without introducing structural changes in it. An example in a virtual classroom are the forums used in block 0, which contain and make known to the student all the information on the course, the resources,

The elaboration strategies, according to the author in reference, constitute an intermediate step between the strictly associative ones, which do not work on the information itself, and the organizational ones, which promote new knowledge structures. In the elaboration, simpler operations can be produced in which some relationships, generally extrinsic, are established between elements of the information that can serve as "scaffolding" for learning through elaboration of meanings and others, more complex, when elaboration occurs. based on the significance of the information elements. An example of these is the construction section that is placed in the academic block of the virtual classroom; there the student finds the truth by his own means and the support of his classmates; the tutor in that section does not interact,

Organizational strategies consist of establishing, in an explicit way, internal relationships between the elements that make up the learning materials and with the prior knowledge that the subject possesses; An example of its use in the virtual classroom is the exhibition section belonging to the academic block, in which all the necessary information that the student should know with the help of videos, files, web page links, among others, is exposed.

Finally, the support strategies are those that, according to the cited author, instead of going to learning the materials, have the mission of increasing the effectiveness of that learning by improving the conditions in which it occurs; An example is the bounce section placed in the academic block; its aim is for the apprentice to assimilate and establish relationships between what they already know and the new learning presented with the help and collaboration of their peers; Among the suggested activities are forums, wikis, chats, videoconferences and blogs, in which knowledge is shared and confrontations are generated regarding the information provided by the tutor.

These conceptions of the different strategies lead us to reflect on the how, with what and why to teach in the virtual educational act, in such a way that, in order to answer these questions and taking into consideration the classification of the strategies of the aforementioned author, it can be deduced that the implicit elements in each of them would be the following: in the organization strategies, the teacher represents the establishment of the necessary structure for the rational systematization of the content, the interaction resources, consultation spaces and the activities of interaction, through the determination of hierarchies, arrangement, correlation and grouping of activities in order to perform and simplify the functions in virtual education.

In associative and preparation, the teacher promotes communication, which includes the time to offer tutoring, interact and evaluate directly; This action is related to the personalization of education, since students are served in the same way in which they seek to link with them so that the methods and techniques used are understood and internalized and the success expected in the program is obtained. process of teaching and learning. This is achieved through interaction between users and the teacher, based on learning and collaborative work so that the evaluation process is a clear and concrete feedback, that encourages comparison and criticality, allows negotiation and supports recovery. From the latter, support strategies are generated in which open motivation,

For his part, Álvarez (2008) states that one of the main advantages of virtual teaching is that it facilitates synchronous and asynchronous interaction, that is, it is not subject to spatial or temporal restrictions. These conditions promote self-regulation of learning, defined by Zimmerman (1990) as those aspects that contribute, in a cognitive-metacognitive, motivational and behavioral way, to the student being an active promoter of their own learning processes. In the cognitive-metacognitive aspect, when they are capable of making decisions that regulate the selection and use of different forms of knowledge: planning, organizing, instructing, controlling and evaluating; in the motivation one, when they are able to have great self-efficacy, self-attributions and great intrinsic interest in the task, highlighting extraordinary effort and persistence during learning; and behaviorally, when they are able to select, structure and create environments to optimize learning, seeking advice, information and places where they can see their learning favored; This is also achieved by promoting collaborative learning. The strengths of this type of learning are based on the use of the aforementioned strategies.

Now, how is this process accomplished in a virtual classroom? One way of promoting the processes of teaching and learning in virtuality is the PACIE methodology, which, according to Oñate (2009), is used in virtual education for the use and application of virtual tools. PACIE means: P, presence (institutional in the internet world); A, scope (both academic, experimental and tutorial); C, training (motivating and preparing teachers in the use of technological tools that reinforce the chairs given); I, interaction (that allows the teacher and student to reach the communication processes of open, permanent and collaborative participation); E, e-learning (facilitates the inclusion of e-learning supported by new technologies, such as Web 2.0, c-learning).

This methodology encourages teachers to structure their classroom taking into account the following blocks: block O, which includes three virtual forums: the first for the information section (general information about the course, objectives and goals, tutor presentation and evaluation processes); the second for the communication section (explains the beginning of each unit, what work will be done in the week, sets dates for evaluations, clarifications and guidelines for student work); and the third presents an interaction section to generate support spaces and positive experiences; it is the foundation of collaborative learning.

The second block is known as the academic one, which contains the exposition section for the presentation of the units and learning contents; the bounce section to create activities necessary for the student to read and assimilate the documents, videos and web links used in the exhibition section; the construction section, in which the student must justify and defend the possible solutions to the topics raised in the course; and the verification section, also called evaluation; Activities that allow knowing if the student learned, assimilated and understood the exposed contents are presented.

The last block is the closing one and contains a negotiation section in the learning community, between tutor and apprentices, directly and indirectly; It includes a feedback section, in which the student generates information in surveys to find out if the interaction, tutor's response and information was correct and significant. The following graph exemplifies the sections mentioned:

The foregoing highlights that the virtual teaching and learning process involves and calls for a tutorial process that considers the design of an interactive virtual classroom and attractive to students, with planning and practicality of strategies that focus on their individual and group needs, in order to foster interaction, the pleasure of learning and the possibility of processing information in a more meaningful way and adapted to the current real social context by promoting collaborative learning.

Collaborative Learning

Panitz (2008) considers collaborative learning as a philosophy of interaction and a way of working that involves the development of both individual knowledge and skills and a positive attitude of interdependence and respect for the contributions of the group. It is a process in which knowledge is discovered by students, reconstructed through concepts that can be related, and expanded through new learning experiences. Hence, collaborative learning highlights the active participation of the student in the learning process because learning arises from transactions between students and between teacher and students.

For her part, Kaye (2003) states that the success of collaborative learning lies in the shared goal, interaction, mutual respect and trust between the members of the group of students, and the creation, manipulation and communication in virtual environments or not. Thus, the basis of collaborative learning in virtual education is cooperation between all the entities involved in the didactic act, which implies working together to promote, enhance and maximize meaningful learning from them.

Among the virtual teaching activities that teachers can use to advise and promote this type of learning are: group chats in the virtual classroom and in another technological medium (Messenger, Skype, Twitter, others), as well as participation in virtual forums and videoconferences , among others. The action of all of them encourages students to participate actively in the discussion of ideas, problems, proposals and projects that lead to a group consensus to solve and solve all the tasks that are defined in the learning activities; In addition, they allow the strengthening of positive relationships between students, high performance and performance in carrying out activities that in themselves involve the self-motivation and motivation of the study group.

In this sense, the role of the teacher that promotes this learning within virtual education is that of a mediator who, according to Díaz and Hernández (2007), specifies and presents the objectives, goals and contents at the beginning of the course; makes decisions about the formation, type, size of groups, and the roles that students will play to ensure interdependence; plans teaching materials with the use of ICT and structures the group goal of positive interdependence; constantly explains and monitors the educational task and the criteria for success through its timely intervention and answers questions and concerns; Evaluate group action and assess the good functioning of the group in general.

Essential Competences Of The Teacher Within Virtual Education

For Camacho (2010), the teacher must have competences that enable him to generate a pedagogical aid that enhances the student's permanence in the virtual course by avoiding the risk of dropping out, increasing their satisfaction and increasing academic achievement; In addition, it must be skillful in technological management that allows a good use of resources and materials and overcome unforeseen events. In this way, some essential competences of the e-learning teacher can be characterized:

- The need to become an intermediary between the student and the institution, to provide information and advice to the system, since credibility in it will initially pass through it.
- Go from being a content expert to a learning mediator, based on experience designs that offer the student an initial structure to start the interaction.
- Possess minimal technical skills not only to intervene in the system, but to resolve the limitations that are presented to the student to interact in it.
- Present the contents of the materials in a way that favors learning to the maximum when their use is individual and solitary, through specific designs, a logical organization of the contents and insertions of bibliography, summaries, concept maps, definitions, diagrams, references to web pages and activities.
- Enhance informative feedback by sending messages via virtual campus based on comments raised by students, such as reflections that arise from the review of papers, clarification of possible doubts and guidance before encountering difficulties.
- Provide sufficient resources to students from materials in different formats to links to web pages, so

that they can respond to demands and activate cognitive learning processes appropriate.

- Propose a learning evaluation process that reveals the result of the construction of knowledge by the student.

- Establish a very large number of interactions with students to collect information about the process and the quality of the construction of knowledge that is produced. These indicators should give the teacher a sufficiently broad perspective on the learning process, so that they can take the initiative and use methodologies and instructional techniques to adequately support each learning process that each student follows.

- Deploy a greater number of aids and see that they are of a different nature, which means greater complexity in your teaching activity, since you will often have to think and develop various ways of presenting the same content and strategically use various semiotic devices, depending on of the needs of the students.

Conclusion

Wondering or wondering about the principles of a pertinent education in this time that one lives, constantly preparing for the future without living or learning from reality, makes one think that an inadequacy is experienced, in which knowledge is disarticulated with reality. More and more knowledge is divided up, while the problems to tackle it are transversal; it is taught to approach an area of knowledge regardless of whether it can be applied in a context. In this sense, today's teacher is called to use ICT as an educational resource that drives the challenge of traveling new paths and experiences in which the teacher and students become jointly responsible for achieving the goals of practical knowledge. through collective self-reflection and self-evaluation.

Thus, it can be affirmed that teaching and learning from virtuality is a highly qualified means for the education of the immediate future, not only as a training space, but as a personalized and collaborative social learning process, with a teaching action that aims to satisfy the needs and interests of the group of students in the search for the development of their abilities through their interaction with the virtual context. All this, through mutual support and collaboration, together with a climate of freedom, tolerance and care in which students live and experience that the educator is also educated, which aims to generate the autonomy and personal independence of the learner, so that it can transform its environment actively and according to the advances that society presents. It, then, It would be the reflection of a proactive, cooperative and dynamic virtual teaching and learning that seeks the educational transformation that the current social context needs. Remember that you teach to learn and you learn to teach.

Google Classroom: the class goes digital

Google offers transversal tools , which can be used for the most common needs, such as organizing daily tasks, planning deadlines and managing your own material (educational or otherwise).

Did you miss the first training pill on Google for Education? Here is the introduction to Google for Education or follow theGoogle Suite for Education course by ANDI - National Association of Italian Teachers.

Today we will talk about Google Classroom . Google's shared cloud 1 classroom reserved for schools. To access it, just enter your credentials and be enabled as an institution or school as explained in the previous guide.

Google Classroom features allow classes to communicate , save time and organize work.

After entering your credentials, you can:

- enroll in a course, an online bulletin board where you can share personalized communications, texts and tests,
- create one from scratch,
- set the permissions (the ability to publish and comment) of other users
- and invite a list of contacts to create your own online classroom.

The possibilities with Google Classroom are numerous, you can ask questions to your class, reuse previously written posts, create an online task or create a communication to be sent directly to pupils' emails.

Its use in everyday life - With Google Classroom, communicating with your students, setting up tasks and making them visible even to colleagues or possible alternates is simple.

Even just sharing an interesting article for your pupils and reading it together the next day without having to print unnecessary sheets that could be lost is easy and intuitive.

Schools need simple, easy-to-use solutions to manage their classrooms. With Google Classroom, teachers are able to assign assignments and tasks to their students in a flash, strengthening communication and relationships between student and teacher.

The direct involvement of students improves as well as the organization and collaboration between the various subjects.

Try to think if for a sudden effort your teaching plan remained incomplete and on your return your students' study programs overlapped with those of the other teachers.

And now try to imagine how easy it would be to organize yourself remotely(also from mobile), assigning tasks and documentation to keep learning constant and to check progress easily from home. Or send notices to remind the most forgetful that you must give your school travel permit by Tuesday and remind your colleagues that you will be absent the next day for a refresher course.

Why is Google Classroom very efficient? Because sharing the slides, notes and in-depth documents of a lesson making them available also to pupils absent for health reasons becomes child's play.

Google has created a centralized work system that becomes a real fundamental tool, indispensable to always keep the attention of our students active.

Each student can check the various deadlines and manage independently, just as the teachers can check in real time who is doing their homework, make suggestions and assign marks.

- Create multimedia content,
- attach files from Google Drive ,
- upload a video,
- insert external links.

they are no longer a difficult task for the less experienced but a simple click from any device with an internet connection.

For a correct use of the Google applications for the school it is possible to enroll in the online course on Google Suite for Education , which provides a complete 360-degree preparation on all the IT tools to be used in the classroom, including Google Classroom. The online course illustrates all the steps and methods of using the multiple functions.

CHAPTER 3: GOOGLE CLASSROOM AND HOME SCHOOLING

Is online learning as effective as face-to-face learning?

Some people believe that courses and exams can only take place when a "real exam" takes students led by a teacher or trainer in a certain place, such as a class. Nothing could be further from reality. So, let's compare these two learning methods.

Face-to-face learning?

Some people believe that courses and exams can only take place when a "real exam" takes students led by a teacher or trainer in a certain place, such as a class. Nothing could be further from reality. So, let's compare these two learning methods.

What are the main benefits of face-to-face learning?

Face-to-face learning has been the norm for centuries.

With face-to-face learning, students interact live with a teacher or instructor. That interaction happens in person, which means that they must be physically present in a classroom to learn. This usually happens on a specific date and time.

Face-to-face learning helps you get organized with your studies, because you have to be present in a place at a specific time. In addition, you can interact with the trainer and other students. If you don't have a lot of self-discipline and don't do your homework, no problem, just sit there and listen to the teacher speaking.

Furthermore, face-to-face learning is more widely recognized as a “real” learning method. Since people have to be physically present for traditional courses, people feel that they are actually taking some time to learn something and they do it seriously. However, teaching in the traditional way does not always guarantee that the person will be more focused or more successful.

Is online learning really effective?

Good question. Even though we are in a modern era where we don't have to be physically present in a place to learn something, people still struggle to take online learning seriously. But let's take a look at the facts

- Most people today prefer to consume content using the internet rather than some other way. The very fact that you are reading this page is proof of this! Why should learning remain strictly traditional while everything else seems to be going in a different direction?

- **Online learning requires more self-discipline - and, surprise! - you can even learn more :** since no teacher supervises you, you have to "supervise yourself". Which means you have to take the time to study, pay attention to what you are studying and apply what you have learned when taking an exam.

- **The exam results showed that those who study remotely can achieve similar or better scores than traditional students in high school and university .** In fact, many of the best universities in the world now offer distance learning courses.

- **No time wasted in traveling:** with online learning, there is no need to spend money and time on transportation. You can study using any internet-connected medium.

- **With online learning, you can still get a diploma or certificate .** Yes, exactly. And that certificate may be the same as those taking face-to-face courses.

So which one should you choose?

Let's not say that traditional learning should be stopped. However, online learning is not only a viable alternative, but an excellent alternative. Some teachers and trainers prefer to use a mixed approach : combining both methods to maximize results.

If you are a teacher or trainer, we recommend that you consider the benefits of online learning and how it can make your life much easier without decreasing quality.

Free Google Classroom for students and teachers: how to use the tool to study at home

The platform helps organize activities and allows you to download files, among other things

Studying at home is becoming easier with the help of technology, an example of this are the **Google** tools , which were made available to all students, teachers and entrepreneurs during this stage of confinement created by coronavirus.

The **technology giant** shared a diversity of courses through the internet to feed education in Mexico.

Such is the case of G Suite and **Classroom** , which according to the Secretary of Public Education, Esteban Moctezuma, were created so that both teachers and students could study for free, in such a way that there was no interruption in their learning, in addition to a benefit for entrepreneurs.

Google Classroom was officially created in 2014 ; However, it took root until this **2020 and gained popularity among students, since they could not attend school classrooms.**

How to use the Classroom tool?

Any person who wants to occupy **Google Classroom** must identify themselves with a **Google or Gmail account** that they must create in order to use said platform.

Then you must enter the internet page classroom.google.com, where you must first check the account with which the interested party is identified, by clicking continue.

Then press the + button located in the upper right where you can **select the class** already created or create a new one. If you write one, the URL address of the class assigned by your teacher will be requested.

Upon entering there are several tabs that will help the student to coordinate and organize their tasks and work.

Files can also be attached **through a link, from the computer, from Google Drive or upload YouTube videos .**

With the tool you can create or select classes. (Photo: Special)

In addition, new participants (students) can be entered and teachers will be able to grade and upload works, allowing remote connection and supervision of students.

What is G Suite?

G Suite is the other Google tool that was designed to control and manage companies with their own domain.

In it you can generate professional email addresses, example your name @ example. com

In April, Google shared one more way to spend time and stay home during this COVID-19 spread period, and offered **classes and courses for small** and medium-sized enterprises (SMEs), so they can develop better learning techniques and overcoming.

The initiative **"grows with Google at home" was aimed at entrepreneurs, business owners, employees, educators, journalists, among others,** who could access some free tools such as Google My Business, which serves to maintain communication with customers.

Through virtual conferences on **YouTube**, the Internet platform offered **three training sessions.**

"The goal of staying connected, improving productivity at work and learning at home, managing businesses remotely and acquiring new **digital skills**, " the company said in a statement.

The virtual courses were some such as: "Free Google tools to help your SME", in which a three-session **course ,** with 35 minutes each, **was offered** , aimed at small and medium entrepreneurs, in addition to Google for Education for teachers, through which teachers learned to implement various teaching materials and strategies.

The implementation of other tools such as: Gmail, Hangouts Meet and Google Drive, Chat, Calendar, Docs was recalled. In addition to tips to use them in the best way.

Virtual education: Advantages, myths and tips to improve results

You may already be convinced that virtual education is an excellent choice for learning and imparting knowledge. Or it may be that you still have your doubts about the effectiveness of this type of education and its scope.

What is a fact is that virtual education continues to gain popularity. **More than six million students currently take one or more online courses ;** 50% of universities offer at least one online program.

... And these numbers will only continue to grow as the incorporation of new technologies continues in today's world.

In a few years, this educational model will be the rule around the world.

Given my career as a leader in university digital transformation, and in the current context in which there are still people who are not convinced about virtual education, I share this article where I list the main benefits, I deny some myths and I offer some good practices to take consider.

Main advantages of virtual education

If you haven't taken an online course yourself, have you ever wondered what the experience of learning virtually is really like? Although the online learning platforms used may differ slightly, virtual education offers many benefits compared to the traditional teaching method, for example:

- **Expanding learning opportunities:** One of the main benefits of virtual education is that it offers a wide variety of resources to the teacher, from virtual visits, online libraries with curated resources, interactive evaluations, connections with experts around the world, etc. With new technologies, classes can be creative and participatory at all times.

- **Learn anywhere:** you only need an electronic device (cell phone, tablet or laptop) to access study materials.

- **You can choose when to study:** many students work; For this reason, **virtual education** allows them to continue learning from anywhere and at any time. A study asked students why do they choose to learn online? Most responded that because of the convenience and flexibility offered by the programs. More than half (59%) of the surveyed students have children, and half reported that they also have a job.

- **Responsibility and autonomy:** creating a routine and carrying out the corresponding activities is good advice for successfully completing the programs offered.

Breaking myths to increase educational reach

Despite the exponential growth of virtual education, many people still consider it an inferior type of education.

I am here to tell you that these beliefs are far from the truth, and that online education can be as credible, reliable, beneficial, and effective as traditional education.

Therefore, I would like to take this opportunity to debunk the 3 most common myths.

Myth 1. The quality of virtual education is inferior.

This is false, because **virtual education** is made up of many quality factors. For example:

- The tutor is a specialist in the areas in which he teaches.
- Technological tools are specialized to provide excellent service.
- Classes are planned through proven and effective educational programs.
- The attention given to the students is personalized.

Myth 2. Teachers are not trained to teach online.

Many times you hear these kinds of unsubstantiated expressions. However, I consider that the demands and challenges of the new knowledge society demand different skills from teachers. The traditional role of the teacher changes in the virtual modality, to become a tutor who facilitates and accompanies the student in their process of building knowledge, respecting their autonomy.

The traditional role of the teacher changes in the virtual modality, to become a tutor that facilitates and accompanies the student in their process of building knowledge, respecting their autonomy.

Myth 3. Virtual education is a fad.

Many people believe that this is a global trend that will soon pass. However, it is false that virtual education is a fad that will disappear over the years.

A key factor for universities to offer online classes is keeping up with new student expectations. In essence, those universities that do not offer virtual education face a competitive disadvantage within a student population that needs and expects to be able to learn online, from anywhere.

The new generations increasingly opt for this learning model. Some of the reasons are:

- Access to education exists for all people, especially for those who work.
- The use of ICT allows student learning and communication to increase , because with the use of mobile devices, digital platforms and / or applications, the information is shared immediately and can be accessed from anywhere.
- With the use of virtual educational platforms, the physical classroom becomes an option. Many of the students who have various activities in their daily lives can access a virtual room where personalized

attention is provided, which allows them to develop their skills and knowledge with higher performance.

Tips to successfully face the challenge of virtual education

Just as virtual education has many benefits, we also face various challenges. Some universities are using innovative methods to foster an online educational experience that is more inclusive, engaging, and responsive to student demands.

Take the following tips into account :

1. **The content created by teachers must be designed specifically for the virtual environment.** Considering that virtual classrooms or online learning courses differ from face-to-face courses, the content must be different too. It is recommended to be shorter and interactive. For example, it is important to offer additional reference materials in certain sections or even external links. This makes the content adaptable to the different needs of the students.

2. **Focus on active learning.** Even the most fun and entertaining teachers can't afford to create passive online lessons. The course should be interactive. A good number of opportunities for student participation should be included, for example combining discussions, collaboration, video and audio clips, and practical exercises with text and possibly short video lectures. No student will remain

attentive and interested for a long time without interactivity.

3. **The "teaching presence" plays a vital role in building a sense of belonging** to the learning community and in keeping students actively interacting with content. Much research has revealed that receiving constant feedback and communication from the teacher can make a big difference in the confidence, motivation and performance of these students in the course.

4. **Students have different learning styles .** In this sense, it is pertinent to identify how their students learn best and thus use different tools to adapt to different styles. I recommend using a mix of various media, including text, video, audio, infographics, presentations, gamification, and more - this has been found to be more effective than including text and audio only.

5. **Segment lessons.** Long 2-3 hour classes with no breaks are probably not the best way to deliver a face-to-face course, and doing this online is even more inefficient. I recommend presenting the information in 10 minute segments and as I mentioned earlier, in varying the format.

With this information, it is possible to improve the scope and results of **virtual education** at all levels.

CHAPTER 4:
TEACHER VIEW

GOOGLE CLASSROOM FOR TEACHERS

The **coronavirus** is causing the number of students who are teaching from home to skyrocket. There are many alternatives for **teaching distance online online** , but one of the most popular in recent days is **Google Classroom**. We explain how to use it and all its details.

Google Classroom was launched in August 2014, and since 2017 it can be used by personal Google accounts without having to have a G Suite subscription. Initially it was designed with the objective of saving paper, but its usefulness has surpassed its initial use to distribute tasks or evaluate content. As its name indicates, it allows to have virtual classrooms, allowing not only teachers and students a more fluid interaction at a distance, but parents can be more informed of the entire educational process. And as we are going to see, it is probably the best tool we have for teaching online, since it also allows us to join Hangouts Meet for video calls and have a complete **virtual classroom** experience .

Creating And Setting Classes

Accessing Google Classroom is really easy. We just have to create access to **classroom.google.com** with our email, either our personal account or one that we have created specifically for classes if we do not want to reveal ours. From there, we will be inside.

In the upper right part we get an icon of "+", in which we can join a class if we are a student, or create a class if we are a teacher. In the case that we are a teacher, it is important that we know that if we are going to teach in an educational center with students, we will have to have an account created for G Suite for Educational Centers, which is free.

To create a class, we can create a class, section, subject, and classroom name. Thanks to this, students can easily identify subjects and classes. From there, we will already have our class created, with the Class Code that we will have to give to the students so that they can get into it.

In the panel we can select the subject of the class, upload a personalized photo, send messages to all students, create class work with tasks and questions and organize the work. We can also manage students and teachers with access from people, and finally also can judge the work of students in the section **Ratings**.

In the section to create jobs we can choose Tasks, questionnaires, questions, materials, etc. We can assign points to each task, and set delivery dates. In the case of the tasks with questionnaires, they can be done using the Google questionnaires.

Inviting your students on Google Classroom

Well hi and welcome to another step by step tutorial on Google Classroom. Last time, we learned how to create a Google Classroom today I.

In this tutorial, we're going to have a look at how to invite students to join your Google Classroom. There are two ways you can invite students into your Google Classroom: by displaying class code, or by inviting them directly.

Well, to invite students by class code, log into your Google Classroom. Select a classroom where you would like to invite your students to. Your class code is displayed right underneath your name, click on Display, make sure that the class code is visible to your students. You can either project it onto the screen or simply write it on the board.

Let's switch over to a student's view to see what they will need to do from there and to be able to use this class code to join your Google Classroom.

Instruct your students to sign into Google using their school Gmail accounts. Instruct your students to go to Google classroom, click the plus button in the top right corner. This is the time where they will insert a class code. Once they finished, click join. That's it, a student has successfully joined your Google Classroom.

Let's now switch over back to teacher's view to see what has changed in our Google Classroom. If you go to people tab you should be able to see students who have successfully joined your classroom. Class code is an easy and straightforward way to invite your students to join a Google Classroom class code doesn't change over time. It is permanent, and it is assigned to Google Classroom. You can use it another time if there are students who were absent while you were displaying the class code.

Direct invitation is another way to populate your Google Classroom. To do that, open your Google classroom, select a class where you would like to invite your students go to "people" tab. Find sign invite students and click on it. This is the field where you will paste or type names or emails of the students who you would like to invite. Once you've finished, click invite. Once the invitation has been sent, you will see a name of the students grayed out. They have received the invitation but have not joined a class yet.

Let's switch over to a student view to see what they will need to do from there and to be able to accept invitation and join your classroom . Instruct your students to login into the Google using their school accounts. Once they've logged in, instruct them to go to Google Classroom. Once there, they should be able to see a Google Classroom, which you have invited them to. In my case, it's my first Google Classroom. Final step they need to take is to click join. That's it. Your student has successfully joined your Google Classroom by direct invitation.

Let's head back over to teachers view to see what has changed and name that used to be grayed out is now solid black. If the name still appears light gray, it means that a student has not yet accepted your invitation.

Well congratulations, you now know how to invite students to join your Google Classroom by class code or by inviting them directly. In our next step, by step Google Classroom tutorials, we'll see how to create and collect assignments from students.

How to create and collect assignments from students

Today, we're going to have a look at how to create and collect assignments. Without further ado, let's get into it.

To create an assignment, go to classwork and click 'Create assignment'. Give your assignment a title, type up instructions for your students. Select whether your assignment will be ungraded, or graded. Select a due date for your assignment. We will talk about topics in another tutorial. So for now, just leave no topics.

There are four kinds of supplementary materials that you can attach to your assignment. The first one is an attachment from your computer or a file, the second one is a file from your Google Drive. The third one is a YouTube video clip. The fourth is linked to any resource found on the internet. For my assignment, I decided to use all four.

To attach files from my computer, I will click on the first icon. Select files from your device, select a file, click Open. Click Upload. Now my assignment has a picture that I attached from my computer.

For a YouTube video clip, I found a clip on 'creativity' that I would like my students to watch. Select the clip that you would like to students to watch and click Add. Now my assignment has a YouTube video clip. But I also have a TED talk that I would like my students to watch. So I will click on the fourth icon(Google drive) copy and paste my link here. Click Add link.

Finally, I would like my students to be able to reflect on all the materials they've watched. For this purposes, I created a Google Doc. So I will click on the second icon and select a Google Doc that I've recently created for this assignment. Select the file from your Google Drive and click Add. One important thing you need to remember when assigning Google Docs to your classes is to select the appropriate sharing type.

There are three types, students can view the file, students can edit the file, and make a copy for each student. Let me briefly describe each one of them. If you select students can view the file then students will only be able to view the Google Doc that you've connected. So in my case, it's not an option because I want them to actually write better reflection. Students can edit the file means that all students will be editing one file in what suits my purposes either because I want each individual student to write his or her own reflection. Third option seems to make more sense ‘make a copy for each student’. The Google Classroom will duplicate this assignment and make a separate copy from

Each student that seems about right before you click Assign, there is still one more feature that we haven't talked about yet multiple assignments. If you are teaching more than one class you can benefit from this feature. Multiple assignment basically means that you assign the same assignment to multiple classes. To do that, scroll up and click for and simply select the classes who you would like to assign this assignment to. So you can also select either all students or you can take individual students. Once you have done all that you can either assign the assignment right away, schedule assignment to be assigned later on all save it as a draft and finalize it later. In my case, I will assign this assignment right away.

Congratulations, you've just created your first assignment,instructions, resources, and student count. It's important to understand what ‘turned in’ and assign means ‘assignment’ means how many students have been assigned this assignment while there are only two students in my

class. So then number two is here, it turned in is how many students have completed and turned their assignments back. And this is what the assignment looks like from your end. But why don't we switch perspective and see what it looks like from students. And now to do that, we're going to imagine that I'm now a student. And I will log into the classroom, log into my Google classroom and see what it looks like. Now to do that, I will open Google, have a login into my Google classroom and select my Google Classroom. When students open their Google Classroom, they immediately log into the stream, which is basically a newsfeed of what is happening and what is new. I can see here that a teacher posted a new assignment, I can also see upcoming due dates. So to open the assignments, I can either click on the assignment in my stream, or I can go to 'classwork' and select my assignment. From here, I can see the assignment name, instructions, all the resources. Well, my assignment is to write a reflection the following topic 'importance of creativity'. Let's imagine that I have access all this resources. And now I'm ready to write by reflection. Well, to do that I open the Google Doc that a teacher has assigned to me previously. You can see from the screen that Google Classroom has created a separate document for me and name it accordingly. Once a student is ready, it's important to turn the assignment back in the 'turn in' button is located in the top right corner. I'm going to click turn in. Google classroom is going to ask me, am I going to turn in this work? Yes, I am going to turn in this work. That's it. My assignment has been submitted.

Now let's jump back to the teacher's side to see what's changed. You can see from my screen that one student has been transmitted into turned in. Now I have one student who has been assigned the assignment but hasn't completed it yet. I also have another student who has completed this assignment and turn it in because this assignment is graded.

My job as a teacher now is to give this assignment a grade and return it to the student. To do that, click on turned in.

This is the name of the student who has completed their assignment, click on the assignment. As a teacher, you have a lot of features when it comes to grading. You can leave a comment, you can suggest new ideas, but this is a topic for another tutorial. Right now we're just gonna look at this assignment. Let's give this student 80 out of 100.

Once you've done that, click return. Confirm your return. That's it. Your job as a teacher is done. You've assigned the work you've marked and return the work. Now let's jump back to students view to see what's changed. As a student I can now see my grade 80 out of 100 there are many other useful features when it comes to grading students work, but we will have a look at them in another section.

So you've learned how to assign, collect and return students work. In our next section, we're going to have a look at how to assign quiz assignments via the Google Classroom.

How To Use Question

Are you one of those educators who would like to engage your students into meaningful and productive online discussions, but you simply don't know where to start, which platform to use which website to go to. And you simply go back to pencil a paper all the time for this kind of assignments. Well, good news. By the end of this section, you will be able to engage your students into meaningful and seamless and authentic online discussions with the help of Google classroom discussion board.

If you're not familiar with Google Classroom, check out previous sections in this book on how to get started. If you have a Google Classroom already, let's dive in.

First thing you need to do is to go to classwork from your Google Classroom homescreen. From there, select Create, select question. This is how we start a discussion board.

First thing we need to think about is what is that that we want our students to talk about. And this is going to be our question. Well, in my case, I want my students to do discuss a video clip I found on YouTube about 'creativity'. I want them to share their insights. So this is going to be my question 'share your insights about the attached video', I'm going to click on YouTube sign and attach the video clip that I would like my students to discuss, share, insights, select the clip, click Add. So I have my question. I have my clip here. And the other thing we need to select is how the students will answer this question. We have two options. We can either accept short answers or multiple choice. Well, in our case, we want to start a discussion board. So short answer makes more sense.

Make sure you enable students to reply to each other. This will enable students to see and reply to each other. Students can edit the answer. I normally leave it on, this option lets students go back and edit the answers after they've been posted in case they've made a typo, they made a mistake, they can go back and edit. Select classes which you want to assign this question to. If you didn't know, you can simultaneously assign the same assignment to different classes to multiple classes. In my case, this is going to be assigned only to my one class. And also you can select students in my case, I have two students. So I'm going to select all students, my assignment is not going to be graded, there'll be no due date, and there'll be no topic. So that said, we all good. We can either ask now, in this case, the assignment will post it right away. We can schedule this assignment for later use, or we can save as draft and maybe ask it later or edit it later. In my case, I'm going to ask it now.

After you've asked your question, it's going to appear onto your classwork or in your stream. This is what the assignment looks like. The question will be right here we have the video clip. And so far, I don't have any one answered. I have two questions. I have two students who have been asked This assignment, but I have no students who have turned it in. So why don't we see what this question looks like from students?

So as a student, this is what it looks like from my end. In my stream, I can see a question that a teacher has posted. I can also go to classwork and see this question there. Let's try and tap it.

This is what the question looks like, I have the question right at the top, and I can do three things. I can add a class comment, I can type my answer, or I can add a private comment. And these three things are slightly different from each other. So why don't we start by typing out answer first an answer to the question. So the question was to share my insights about the video attached. So my insight would be this video is great. I'm going to click turn in. And you will notice that once I've turned in, I can now see classmate answers if I click on see classmates answers I can see only my answer so far. I can also see how many replies I have right here. I have zero replies so far. Now let's try and add a class comment which will look different from answer to the question. So my class comment is going to be, 'this is an awesome assignment', clicking right there. I can also add a private comment, a private comment as opposed to class comment, and my answer will only be viewable by my teacher. If I add a private comment, I can say 'this is my private comment to a teacher', click on this button here. I'm using Google Classroom app on this iPad, which looks a little bit different from the time when you use Google Classroom in the internet browser.

Alright, so what we've done so far, we've added our answer. We've added a class comment, and we've added a private comment. Let's now see what it looks like from another student's account. The same options available to me I can add a class comment I can tell my answer I can add a private comment. And you can notice that I already have one class comment which was made by another student. 'This is an awesome assignment'. I don't see his private comment which went to a teacher. So I'm going to type my answer first to be able to see answers from all the students. 'I think this video is outdated'. This is my opinion. So once I've done that, click turning. You notice that now I can see classmates answers if I tap on classmate answers, I can now see my answer, which is MSCI two I think this video is outdated, but I can also see answer from another student, Ms one iPad one 'This video is great'. And what I can do, I could click on reply sign and start a discussion. My reply would be 'I like your idea', post it. You can go back to the first student, I can now have one reply and I can click on this reply and see the response from another student. This is how you can initiate discussions. If I go to my tutor's account, I can now see that I have two students who have turned in the assignment I can see one class comment here. If I tap on view answers. I can see the private comments right under the student's name by tapping student one, a student who has private comment. This is my private comment to the teacher, I can reply privately. 'Thank you for your private Comment'. This comment will go directly to this student. This is how communication between you and a student and among students will look like when you initiate Google classroom discussion board.

There's still one thing you can do to have a little bit more control over the students. If you'd go to student answers and click on three dots. You can mute those students. Muted students can still submit work but other students won't see it cannot reply to classmates, they can comment on posts. You see what is going on here. If some of the students start making silly posts, and making silly remarks, you can just mute them and they'll be working by themselves. They won't be able to see anyone's work. They won't be able to interfere, they'll be working just by themselves but do you still will be able to collect their assignment. So this is a kind of a moderation you can integrate with Google classroom discussion board.

Alright, the last thing I want to leave you with is sometimes students confuse class comment and answer to the question. What I personally do I disable class comments, because when you start a discussion board, it's a little bit confusing for the students whether they should post a class comment or whether they should answer the question. So I normally disable those class comments and the discussion board goes much much more smoothly. Well, to disable class comments, go to your Google Classroom home screen, click on the gear button, scroll a little bit down to stream, students can post and comment and select 'only teachers can post and comment' and click Save. As a teacher I'm still able to post class comments, but students can only either answer the question or add a private comment or reply to other students posts. Now you know all the steps to start discussing boards on Google Classroom.

In our next Google classroom, step by step video tutorials, we'll have a look at the best way to share materials and resources with your students.

How to Use Rubrics

Today, we're going to look at the brand new feature of the Google Classroom rubrics. Google has announced this feature recently, and at the time of the recording, it's still under development, the access has been given to some testers, and I've been fortunate enough to be one of them. So I'm super excited to share with you what Google has prepared for us. If you're reading this section when this feature has been released, then you're lucky one and you can just follow along with me. If you're reading this section when this feature hasn't been released, well just see it as a head start to get ready when it will become available.

So without further ado, let's have a look at the brand new feature of Google Classroom - Rubrics.

If we go to assignment, you will see a new sign has been added to the user interface to the right of the topic. First thing you need to do is create a title because I don't have any rubrics, I'm going to create a rubric from scratch.

I'm going to be using this rubric for grading student essay. So my first criteria is going to be word choice. I'm going to assign three points for level three. And this is going to be a description, accurate use of vocabulary. For the sake of time, I'm going to keep my description very simple. My second level is going to cost two points is going to be level two, and the description will be average use of vocabulary. My third level is going to give student one point, it's going to be level one, and the description will be poor use of vocabulary. To add a level we click on the plus button to the leader level, we need to click on three dots and delete level.

So my first criteria is ready, I can add a new criteria and if I click that, a new field will be generated for another criteria or what I can do I can duplicate this criteria and just change word choice. I will change it to grammar and tweak my description a little bit at first description will be accurate use of grammar

The second description is going to be average, I can duplicate the grammar and choose 'Opinion'. First level is going to work for point, then three, two and one. Google rubrics automatically generate the top score. I have three points in word choice, three points in grammar, and four points and opinion, which gives me 10 points. Once my rubric is ready, I'm going to click Save.

Once you save the rubric, it will be viewable in the assignment, you can click on the rubric, this is what it will look like. You have an option to clear the criteria, expand them one by one or expand them all at once. Once your assignment is ready, click 'assign' . The assignment has been generated. Why don't we take a look at this assignment and rubric from the students end.

So as a student, I can see that a teacher has posted a new assignment I can see my stream or I can go to my classwork and see from their assignment for test of hooby first I noticed when I opened this assignment is that it has a rubric. If I click around the rubric, there's nothing I can do really. But this, the rubric is a good way to let your students know what is expected of them. I know what I need to do to get 10 my I need to make sure that my vocabulary is accurate, my grammar is accurate, and I don't have a description for opinion, but they should be there. So why don't we try and submit our work so a teacher can graded we're going to imagine that the assignment for rubric is my essay.

Now my assignment is turned in, and it's time for a teacher to market. So from the teacher screen, click on 'turned in' and see the student's submission. This is the student who has submitted his work as a junior I can now use the rubric I created for this assignment to mark students work to simultaneously view students work and mark it with the rubric. I need to click on grading tool. My rubric will appear on the right hand side of my screen. I can expand each level and market accordingly. So what we've done right now we've looked at students work, and we've marked it at the same time using our rubric, you will notice that Google rubric has generated the total score of seven out of 10. Based on the levels that we have selected. What it didn't do, however, it didn't transfer the rubric score into the grade. The Google's rubric automatically transfer score of the rubric on to the final grade.

So once we've done that, as usual, we're going to click return and the work will be returned to the student. So let's go back to the students view to see what has changed from their perspective. I can click on the rubric and see where my score from. My word choice earned two points, my grammar earned me two points, in my opinion, are my three points for the total of seven. I cannot see a final score of the rubric, it should be seven out of 10 here. And I can also see my final score of 70 out of 100.

I'm super excited to share this feature with you. And I think this has a great potential to streamline a student's workflow, increase the transparency in terms of expectations, and where does the score come from. It's just a really nice addition to the Google Classroom.

CHAPTER 5:
STUDENT VIEW

Google Classroom For Students: Accessing Google Classroom

On this page you will find the instructions to perform the **first operations in Google Classroom:** access, view assignments and materials, return assignments to the teacher. Classroom allows you to perform many other operations: refer first of all to your teachers, who will show you the right working method for your class. You can also find many online tutorials that explain all Classroom functions in a simple way; some are also indicated at the bottom of this page.

As always, accessing from a computer or smartphone/ tablet is slightly different. Here are different indications according to the device you use .

If you use tablets or smartphones, first read the From Computer section , which explains all the steps and ways in which to perform the various operations in Classroom; then look at the From mobile section , where you will find only the differences compared to the computer screens.

FROM COMPUTER

Log in to Classroom

- use the Chrome browser
- go to google.it
- make sure you're signed in with your G Suite account, or sign in
- click at the top right on the icon with the 9 dots and choose Classroom
- if you don't find the icon, you can type directly into the classroom.google.com address bar
- when you enter Classroom you will see all the courses to which your teachers have added you: they are organized as large independent squares
- to participate in a course you must accept the invitation from the teacher. When you see a course with the blue Subscribe button , click it; if you don't see that button, it means that you are already registered:

Entering the course: materials and tasks

To enter the course just click on the course title, inside the right box. In the screen that opens you can find tasks and materials in two different ways. If you look up, you see the two Stream and Jobs tabs of the course :

In the Stream tab - the one that appears to you first when you enter the course - you find the teacher's homework, materials and comments in reverse chronological order.

As in social networks, you will find the latest things at the top, and as you go down you will find the previous ones. So if you want to see new assignments or materials, this card is the most suitable.

On the right you have a box that reminds you if you have tasks that are about to complete.

In the Works tab of the course you will find the same materials and tasks (not the comments and announcements instead), but in different order: they are ordered in the way the teacher decided, and can be grouped by topics.

If you want to search for a material or assignment by topic, this tab can be more useful because it is better organized.

Look at the materials

The activities that teachers give you are called in two different ways in Classroom: **materials** and **assignments** . Materials and assignments contain very similar activities, they have one important difference:

- when a teacher assigns you **materials** , you just have to open them and do what you find in the instructions
- when a teacher assigns you **tasks** instead, in addition to opening them and doing what you find in the instructions, **you have to return them** , otherwise the task is not performed; see below how to do it

To **open a material or a task ,** just click on it. You can do this from the Stream tab or the Course materials tab , it doesn't change. You find instructions that tell you what to do, and very often you find attachments that you need to read, study, complete ... according to the indications of your teachers.

If you **open a material** , you simply find instructions and attachments. Follow the directions, consult the attachments, then you don't have to do anything else.

Do your homework and return it

If you **open a task** you do the same things seen for the material: at the end, however, **you have to deliver it .** You find two **different keys depending on the type of task** that the teacher has given you.

1. If you need to complete a Google **Document in the task, you will** see a screen like this:

To do your work - in this example complete the table - click on the right, in the Your work column , above the document icon: the document will open in a new Chrome tab. When you have completed the document, you must neither save (save yourself) and **you must not click on the blue Share button .** Instead, you must **click on Delivery .**

Confirm that you want to deliver in the box that appears: in this way the teacher received your assignment.

2. If, however, there are no Google documents to complete **in the task** , but other types of attachments to work on, a slightly different screen appears:

In this case, after having done the task following the instructions, just click on Mark as completed (with the next confirmation), and the task is returned.

Add more files to the assignment

It may happen that you need to **add more files to the assigned task .** For example, the photo of the exercises you did on the book. Or you have to make a new document to write a text, and so on. To add a file, look to the right in the Your work column , and **click on the Add or create button.** By clicking on it, this menu appears:

If you need to add a file that you have already created (for example the photo of the exercises, the audio file with the execution of the instrument piece, or any other attachment) click on File if you have to upload it from your computer or mobile device, otherwise choose Google Drive if you already uploaded the file to your Drive. You can also create new files directly from here, choosing one of the last 4 items. You can attach multiple files by repeating the operation several times. When you have attached what you need, click on Delivery .

FROM A MOBILE DEVICE

Log in to Classroom

From smartphone or tablet do not use the browser (Chrome or others): you must use the Classroom app. **Before** using the app you need to **add the G Suite account to your device** from the settings; if you need you can follow the instructions of the dedicated guide . Install the Classroom app from the Play Store or the App Store. When you open the app, check that the G Suite account is selected, and not your personal Gmail or other accounts; if you need, follow the instructions in the dedicated guide .

Entering the course: materials and tasks

Everything as from a computer, with the only difference that the icons for switching from Stream to Course work are located at the bottom instead of at the top.

Look at the materials

No difference from the computer.

Do your homework and return it

Everything as per computer. The only difference is this: to display the column Your work , which contains the buttons Delivery or Mark as completed , you must click the triangle that you see below. After clicking it, you see all the options in the column.

From a mobile device, when you click on Add attachment you have a few more options: you can take photos or record videos directly from there, without having to prepare them first. So **if you have to attach the photo of the exercises,** for example, you can skip a step by photographing them **directly from within the task ,** choosing Add attachment > Take photo .

Basic Guide To Google Classroom For Students

The Google Classroom interface is simple. Teachers can create a page for each class and then invite their students. Through the platform you can send and schedule messages to all students (or just a group).

One of the most useful functions is the one that allows you to create educational materials. You can help yourself with other tools such as Documents, Presentations and Spreadsheets. You will also have at your fingertips a shared folder on Google Drive.

1. Menu

Here you will find a calendar, a to-do list, your classes and much more.

2. Plank

This is where you will see the communications between students and teachers.

3. Class work

You will be able to create educational materials, assign homework and ask questions of the class.

4 people

All the information related to the students who are part of the class is saved. You can remove a student from the virtual class whenever you want.

5. Ratings

With Google Classroom you can also make a note of the tasks.

6. Class settings

You can change the class settings and easily access other Google services.

7. Class code

Students must enter this code to join the class.

8. Topic

You can customize the interface of each class with a file image or your own.

9. Next delivery date

Students will find here a list of all pending homework.

10. Publications

You can share files, links, and assignments with the class.

GOOGLE CLASSROOM FOR STUDENTS

How To Join And Participate & The Four Types of Assignments

In this section, you're going to learn how to use Google Classroom as a student. To use Google Classroom.

First thing you need to have is a Google account. So head over to google.com. And sign in if you already have an account, or create a new one. After you've signed in or created an account, click on Google Apps, scroll all the way down and choose Google Classroom.

Welcome to your Google Classroom class list. This is where you will see all the classes that you've enrolled in. There are two ways to join a new class. First, if your teacher has given you a class code, click on the 'plus' sign and click 'Join class'. Enter the class code that your teacher has provided you with. If your teacher has invited to you via email, you will see an invitation to join the class. It will look something like this with a class name, your teacher's name, teacher's Avatar and two options decline and join. Choose join.

Welcome to your Google Classroom homescreen. First is your 'stream'. This is where all the announcements and all the new assignments will appear once a teacher has posted them. Right now, there are four posts and there's one announcement. On the left hand side you see upcoming events and due dates. At the top, you see three tabs 'stream'. The thing we're looking at right now, classwork, and people people stab will contain lists of teachers who are teaching this class and also your classmates.

Most of the time you'll be working from 'classwork' tab, which will contain posts or assignments from your teacher. Teachers can post four different kinds of assignments. First type is a simple assignment. The second type is a quiz assignment. The third one is a question. And finally there is a material. Now let's have a look at each type in more detail. If your teacher has created an assignment, it will most likely contain the following things. First, there's a name of the assignment right now it's just an assignment. If there's a due date, the due date will appear on the right. Next, there is a list of instructions, a rubric and supporting materials. What I'm going to do as a student is follow teachers instructions. My first instructions is to read article titled 'transforming education in Minecraft'. Now the article is right here to read the article, simply click on it. This will open a new window, which you can use to read the article. The second task is to use document titled personal reflection to express my thoughts. The teacher has also provided me with a document for my personal reflection and teacher has also provided me with a rubric, which I can use to see what kind of word choice, grammar and structure I need to use to score maximum number of points. I'm going to use this rubric to write my personal reflection.

To write personal reflection, click on the file. Once you've clicked on the file, tab will be open. This is a Google Doc, which you will use to write your reflection. Let's assume that I finished my reflection. And I'm ready to turn in my work. So what I'm going to do is click 'turn in' and Google Classroom warns me that if I'm ready to submit my assignment, I will click turn it. But I think there is one more assignment from my teacher, so I'm not going to turn in my assignment. For now, I will go back to my assignment and reconstruction 'record and submit a short video blog or podcast about how I use video games for educational purposes'. For this task, I don't have a template, I don't have a file or an article to read. I actually need to create an upload something. To do that click on View assignment. Because we've already completed our reflection, our reflection is right here on our work, but we haven't turned in our work yet, meaning that our teacher won't be able to see it yet. Because we still have one more step.

Let's assume that I've recorded my podcast. And now I'm ready to upload this onto the Google Classroom. To upload files onto the Google Classroom, click Add or create. Then choose where your files are stored Google Drive or link from the internet or files. In my case, I have files on my computer. So I'm going to click files, select files from my device and select files that I would like to upload. In this case, I have one audio file, I have one picture and my video blog. I'm going to select all three, click open, and then upload. Google Drive will take a couple of seconds to upload my files onto the Google Classroom. Now once I'm finished, I'm going to be brought back to my Google Classroom screen.

Now I have more files under my work. I have my reflection I have

Have my audio file, I have my picture, and video block. The number of the files will vary depending on the instructions of your teacher, but do know that you can submit different kinds of media: files, audio files, pictures, and even video files. Once you're ready to turn in your work, click 'turn in', Google Classroom will ask you one more time whether you would like to submit this files as your response. If you are sure 'click turn in'. Now when our assignment has been turned in, it's time for your teacher to view your assignment and give you the grade.

After the teacher has returned your work, a couple of things have changed. First, you've been given a final grade that has been generated from the rubric. Remember how we saw this rubric before the assignment. Now your teacher has marked your level to see where you landed in each criteria, click on expand. The teacher has also left you at private comment. A private comment is a comment that only you can see. If you would like to respond to your teacher, you can do so using 'add private comment' feature.

We've looked at assignment and how we can submit different kinds of files to respond to our teacher's assignment. Our assignment is now graded. So let's move on to another type of assignment, which is quiz assignment. Once you click on the quiz assignment, as usual, you will see a due date, you will see your teachers instructions, and you will also see a quiz, which is a Google form. To complete the quiz, click on the Google Forms. Once you click on the Google Forms Google Classroom will take you to the quiz. A Google quiz can contain different kinds of questions. The first two are multiple choice. Our third question has checkboxes so they can be more than one correct answer.

Our final question is an open-ended question which means you need to type in your answer.

Once you've completed the quiz, make sure that you click 'Submit' button. Now your assignment has been turned in, and it's time for your teacher to grade it and return it back to you. Once a teacher has graded and returned your work back to you, you will see your score right here.

Let's go ahead and look at another type of assignment, which is question. Question type of assignment usually contains a question and maybe some supporting materials. In this case, a teacher has set instructions to watch the trolley problem video clip, which is attached to the question, and then write an answer to the question 'what would I do in this situation?' Let's imagine that I viewed the clip and I'm ready to answer the question. To answer the question, click on View question. type your answer right here, under 'type you answer'. Once your answer is ready, click 'turn in'. Google Classroom will ask you whether I'm sure I want to turn in because I won't be able to make changes to my answer. Once I've solved man, I'm sure and I'm going to turn in a teacher has always instructed me to respond to at least two of my classmates. You might have noticed that once I've submitted my answer, I can now see my classmate comments and respond to them. So I'm going to click see classmate comments and respond to them. My name is Ms three iPad three, and Ms. One iPad one has posted an answer. To reply to your classmate click 'reply'.

My comment or response is now recorded on their ms one iPad one. This is my response to my classmate, other students might reply to your answer. So make sure you check on the discussion board and have a productive discussion with your classmate.

Let's head back to our class and have a look at the final type of assignment which is material. Unlike question or quiz assignment for simple assignment, material does not require your submission. In other words, you don't need to submit anything in the material. In this case, a teacher has assigned a material and the instructions are use the material to review for the upcoming test on Monday, and the material is a link to a khanacademy video clip. If you click on View material, the only thing you can do is add a class comment. No other actions apart from viewing the clip is required.

Let's see what you've learned today. We've learned how to join Google Classroom either by class code or direct invitation by your teacher. We also looked at four different kinds of assignment: assignment, quiz assignment, question and material. We've also learned how to respond to each kind of assignment.

CHAPTER 6:
EXTENSION AND APPS

The 13 Best Must-Have Google Chrome Extensions for Teachers

In this section, I'm going to show you 14 must have Google Chrome extensions for teachers. The right combination of Google Chrome extensions can help you organize materials, can help you more effectively deliver instruction, and can also make what you present to students more fun and engaging. Whether it's recording screen capture video tutorials for students, drawing and annotating directly on the computer screen you're projecting ,pushing websites out to student computers, auto translating webpages to other languages, or helping you easily save and organize webpages, images and files in the right place. Google Chrome extensions will power up your internet browser and make your life as a teacher just a little bit easier.

First, it's important to note that in order to use Google Chrome extensions, you need to be using the Google

Chrome internet browser. All of the extensions I'm going to show you can be found in the Google Chrome store, and you can download them for free. So let's go ahead and head over to the Google Chrome store to check it out. As you will see, there are tons of different Google Chrome extensions that you can add to power up your browser and customize it and pretty much any way you want you can see up here on my Chrome browser that I've already added a bunch of different Chrome extensions. Once you've installed them. You can drag and drop them wherever you want to change the order. And if you want to delete an extension that you added, just right click and hit Delete. Okay, there are tons of different Chrome extensions.

And I only have time here to focus on the most impactful Chrome extensions that you can have for your life as a teacher.

1. Screencastify

The first and I think most important Google Chrome extension that you need to have is screencastify. Screencastify allows you to easily make video tutorials for your students that you can then post to your digital classroom, such as Google Classroom. Once you've created a video tutorial, students can watch them at their own pace, they can watch videos outside of class, and I promise once you start using it, it's going to completely transform the way that you teach.

For this first extension, I'm going to walk through the entire process of how you would install it on your browser. When you're ready to add the extension, click Add to Chrome, click Add extension. And in this case with screencastify, you're going to be asked to quickly set up an account the first time that you use it. So let's Let's say that I'm in a program like Book Creator, and I want to teach my students how they're going to use it. All I do is go up to the screencastify extension, click on it, click record, and it's going to start recording a screen capture of what I am doing on the screen, as well as my voice and even a video of myself if I choose that option. Once you're ready to stop the video, click the extension again, and then click stop. And there you'll be given a bunch of different options. If you want to share the video to Google Classroom directly, to a YouTube channel that you've created, or to your Google Drive. You can do any of those with your video.

2. TabScissors

The next extension that you need is called tab scissors. Once you have tab scissors installed, it will allow you to evenly split two tabs that you have on your browser, so they're both visible on the screen. Tab Scissors can be incredibly helpful if you're trying to enter grades in your gradebook from assignments on a separate page on Google Classroom, or if you're trying to enter names into a website from a class list that you have pulled up on a Google sheets. In order to put those tabs back together, you're going to want to get a third extension called tab glue.

3. Tab Glue

After you've installed tab glue, all you have to do is click that extension, and it will glue the two tabs that you just separated back together.

4. Web Paint

Another essential Google Chrome extension is called web paint. If you project your computer screen a lot in class web paint is absolutely going to change your life. So let's say you're projecting a website like Newsela, and you want to emphasize the title of an article, just click on the web paint icon, click on the drawing tool. You can change the size and color and then you can draw freely all over the webpage that you're projecting for students. It turns every web page that you project into something that is totally customizable for you to write on however you would like.

There are other cool tools like Color Fill, you could draw a box around the title of this article and then fill the rest of the background into just really emphasize the articles title for students. web paint is amazing. It's a tool that I use on almost a daily basis now in my classes

5. Share To Classroom

The next extension that I'm going to show you share to classroom is an extension that I use on a daily basis. And if you're a Google Classroom user, it's an extension that you absolutely must have. In order for the share to classroom extension to work, students do also need to have that extension installed on their browsers. Once they have it installed. You can push websites out to them at any time during class, they don't even need to be logged into their Google Classroom.

So let's say I want to share this article to my students about the Great Pacific Garbage Patch. All I have to do is click the Share to classroom icon then click the push button. And that website will show up immediately on students computers in my class. Rather than having to get everybody's attention back and say, hey, I want everybody to go to this other web page. All I do now is click push to students and that website pops up for all of my class. It's really a game changer.

In addition to pushing an assignment out to students, you'll see that you can also take that webpage and make it an assignment, make it a question or a resource that you're going to post to Google Classroom.

6. Google Keep

The next two extensions helped me organize my materials and streamline my workflow. I'm a Google Keep user, I use Google Keep as an online sticky note system, rather than a paper to do list to track all the different things that I need to do. Google Keep is great, because you can also share it with other people like your students. And one way that you can use it in class is to make a collaborative list of different resources on a topic.

So let's say that you have a shared Google Keep sticky note and you find a resource that you like that you want to add to a list, simply click the Google Keep extension. And then if you want, you can add a title and a label if you're creating new one. And you'll see when you go back to Google keep that you now have a label with that specific resource on it.

7. Save to Google Drive

For similar purposes, I also recommend that you get the Save to drive extension. Once you have the Google Drive extension installed anything that you right click can now be auto added to your Google Drive. So let's say you find a picture that you like, rather than downloading it to your computer and then re uploading it back to your Google Drive, you can now save that image directly into your Google Drive folder to streamline your workflow and make your life just a little bit easier. After you've saved it, you'll see that you can change the destination for where it goes into your Google Drive. And you can also change the default settings if you want everything to consistently go in the same place.

8. One Click Full Page Screenshot

Next, I recommend that you get the screenshot extension. So let's say that you have found a resource that you want or you are looking at a student's project and you want to screenshot that to upload it to Google classroom or to a class website. All you need to do is click on screenshot and it will produce an instant screenshot of that page. You'll see at the bottom there are also different annotation tools if you want it to modify it, and then you can click download to open up the screenshot.

9. Google Translate

Next, I recommend that you get the Google Translate extension. Google Translate is extremely powerful, and will allow you to auto translate anything that is in front of the screen. So let's say that I need to translate this website into another language for one of my students, all I need to do is go up to the Google Translate extension, click translate this page, select a language that I want to translate to. And there you'll see that the webpage is now fully translated into Spanish. This also applies to Google Docs. So if you have a document that you need to translate quickly, and you need to share that with families or students, same thing, click Google Translate, select a language and you'll see that it's been auto translated. Now of course, the translation is not 100% perfect, but it's a great option if you need to improve your communication with students and families who speak another language.

10. Google Calendar

Next for my own personal organization and sanity, I like to have the Google Calendar extension out into my browser. Once you have the extension added, you'll see that it tells you how much time you have until your next scheduled event. You can also click on the calendar extension to see your overall schedule for the day. I find it really helpful to just have a quick glance at what I'm doing without having to go and open up my calendar in a separate tab.

11. Small PDF

Next, I'm going to show you small PDF and this one might blow your mind a little bit. Small PDF is a Google extension that will allow you to auto convert any document from one format to the other. That's right, let's say you have a PDF and you just want to quickly convert it into a Word doc. You can use small PDF to do exactly that. So the way it works is that you click on small PDF, choose the type of file that you want to convert to and from, then you'll see it takes me to a web page where I'm going to drag the file that I want to convert in, click 'Convert to word' it will convert your document and now I have an editable document out of a document that I previously was unable to edit. You can also go the other way around and convert a Word document into a PDF, or choose from a variety of other types of formats.

12. Bitmoji

The last two Google Chrome extensions that I'm going to show you are really just about adding a little bit more joy factor to your classes. The first is the bitmoji extension. Now it is important to mention that you need to set up bitmoji on iOS or Android in order to be able to use it. Once you've signed up and created a bitmoji account, you can click on the extension and then choose from a wide variety of avatars of yourself doing different things and saying different things that you can drop into Google Slides or into emails or documents to make them a little bit more fun and engaging in addition to bitmoji.

13. Giphy

I also really liked using the Giphy Chrome extension With Giphy, you can select from a wide range of different animated gifs and once you found one that you like, all you have to do is drag and drop it into a slide or a document. Again, just to make that a little bit more fun and engaging for students.

There are clearly an enormous amount of Google Chrome extensions. But I think these 13 are the most important for teachers in terms of helping you streamline your workflow, present information more effectively for students, and also add a little bit of joy factor to the work that you present to your class. I'm sure many of you have other suggestions about awesome Google Chrome extensions for teachers.

The 12 Best Google Classroom Apps

Google Classroom has become a must-have tool for teachers. This free resource allows educators to assign work, track progress, and communicate with students and parents online. Make your Google Classroom experience even better with these apps and websites, all of which integrate seamlessly with your online classroom. Most are completely free; a few offer paid options, but their free versions have plenty of fantastic free features worth exploring.

1. CK-12

You won't believe the incredible amount of free resources available on CK-12. Every subject, every grade ... it's all covered in videos, exercises, lessons, and even complete textbooks. It's a cinch to assign any of these items in Google Classroom, and completion and grades are recorded in your online Gradebook. (Web)

2. Edpuzzle

Turn any video anywhere into an interactive lesson, or even upload your own. Add questions, audio, or notes, so students can watch and learn at their own pace. The tracking features allow you to monitor their progress and comprehension, and integrate easily with Google Classroom. The robust free plan includes storage for up to 20 videos at a time. (Web, iOS, and Android)

3. Explain Everything

Explain Everything is a whiteboard app, and you can use it just as you would an interactive whiteboard in the classroom. Even better, it allows you to record your interactions and share them via Google Classroom for students to view later. The free version has some limitations but provides plenty of cool features; premium education plans are available . (Web, iOS, and Android)

4. Flipgrid

With Flipgrid, students record short videos to respond to topics you assign. This is an especially cool app for students who are hesitant to speak up live on Zoom calls; it gives everyone a chance to be heard. It's easy to share your grids and assignments with Google Classroom. (Web, iOS, and Android)

5. Google Cast for Education

This simple Chrome extension makes it a breeze to share your screen with anyone. In a classroom setting (in-person or virtual), students share their screen to the teacher, and the teacher shares it with the class using a projector or through Google Classroom. It's simple, free, and a must for every user. (Web)

6. Khan Academy

Many teachers are already familiar with Khan Academy's incredibly wide range of free online learning resources. They cover every subject and grade level, and give students the extra practice they need to master important concepts. Create and integrate classes using your rosters from Google Classroom and you're all set to assign content. (Web, iOS, and Android)

7. Listenwise

Each day, Listenwise posts a new free current events podcast you can share with your students. These short audio lessons are great for morning meetings or starting general current events discussions. Listenwise Premium offers a large podcast library with lessons, quizzes, and interactive transcripts, currently free to try for 90 days. (Web)

8. Quizizz

Quizizz is a nifty tool for helping students review what they're learning in class. Use one of the thousands of quizzes already available, or create your own. Host live online quiz games in class, or assign them as homework using Google Classroom. Customize each assignment to indicate how many times a student may attempt each question, and whether they see the correct answers when they're done—instant feedback that makes learning more meaningful. (Web, iOS, and Android)

9. Quizlet

This is one of the most popular online flashcard apps, and it's entirely free. Find the flashcards you need in their extensive library, or create your own to support any kind of lesson. Share the flashcards to Google Classroom to give students instant access to these practice tools in school or at home. (Web, iOS, and Android)

10. Science Buddies

This site is every science teacher's best friend. It's packed with free videos, lesson plans, and experiments, all searchable by grade level and subject. This is also a terrific go-to during science fair season, with scientific method resources galore, science fair planning tools, and an enormous repository of project ideas. When you use Science Buddies with Google Classroom, you get access to extra quizzes and assessments too. (Web)

11. Wakelet

Think of Wakelet as a collaborative tool for organizing and sharing information. Use it to create and share lessons with your students by collecting media all in one place, with your own notes and explanations. Even better, have students use it to create presentations, book reports, newsletters, and more right in Google Classroom. (Web, iOS, and Android)

12. Workbench

Workbench is a collection of shareable lessons and videos on all sorts of topics. Find and assign existing lessons, or create your own for a customized experience. Embed videos, provide instructions, and even lay out entire projects for students to complete with the resources on this free site. (Web)

CHAPTER 7: OTHER AMAZING THINGS ABOUT GOOGLE CLASSROOM

Ten Reasons Why You Should Use Google Classroom

If we could offer teachers something that would save them time, save money at school, better communicate with students and parents, help struggling students, and impact the learning environment for students ... could you consider using it? I suppose they would.

If you've been using Google Classroom for the past few years, you probably already know why using it is good. But if it's new to you, you probably want to know the reasons why this change is a good fit for students. Here are some things to consider:

1. **Google Classroom is easy to use .** Compared to other LMS (Learning Management Systems) or "Learning Management Systems" that have been popular in the last decade, Google Classroom is incredibly simple.

Creating a new classroom does not take much time or experience. Our technical team trained for an hour, and all of us had a classroom set up and running at the end of the session.

2. **Google Classroom helps you communicate more efficiently.** You enter student email addresses only once, and communication in the classroom is done. Simply by entering the student in the classroom, the teacher has an email group, a discussion group and an automatically created Google Calendar. Plus it's easy to add and remove students from the class if needed.

3. **Google Classroom helps you communicate more effectively.** Probably more important than being easy to use and efficient, communication tools are also very effective. Because everything is cloud-based, there is no more "loss" of assignments by students. If a student is absent, communication is perfect. Last month, Google Classroom added a parent notification feature to keep parents informed of what's happening in the "classroom."

4. **Google Classroom is more profitable and is better for the environment.** Personally, I'm not completely "sold" on paperless learning, especially for younger students. But I do see a real advantage in making schools more profitable when it comes to copying and printing. If every student has a device that connects to the Internet, every sheet of paper that we keep only

makes the school more efficient and environmentally responsible.

5. **This is how students will continue to learn in the future .** College campuses no longer expect junior students to print their five-page essays. As K-12 teachers, we must take note and prepare our students for the world in which they will be living.

6. **It's best for struggling students ...** as long as you help them manage the device. (The device itself can be a distraction at times, so management needs to be taught.)

   The reason Google Classroom is better is because of the organizational advantage it gives them. Assignments are never lost and each class is already organized by the teacher. However, for these students, navigating this has to be taught. Although students are digital natives, it does not mean that they understand how adults organize their world to help them learn.

7. **With Google Classroom, collaboration is easier outside of school (i.e. Flipped Classroom).** Again, it is cloud based and accessible from anywhere with a connection. Students can share assignments and work from home together to complete them. Collaboration is not just limited to working in groups with other colleagues. A teacher can turn the classroom by sharing a video so that it can be seen later, in this way they can prepare for the questionnaire the next day. The possibilities are endless.

8. **Teacher planning is easy, and the initial time is worth it .** More new features in Google Classroom allow teachers to schedule homework in the future. Designated assignments could be scheduled to take place live on a Monday and then close on Friday. If a teacher is on an extended absence, the teacher may schedule assignments. Google Classroom can also be used from semester to semester and from year to year. It would be terrible for a teacher to simply copy and paste a Google Classroom for the next group of students, but it does save time as it allows you to have certain things already in place (class schedule, expectations ranking, etc.).

9. **By incorporating forms, feedback is instantaneous and usable.** One of my teachers was having students complete a multiple choice questionnaire while watching the video. This increases engagement and accountability, but also allows the teacher to see the results at the end of the video. In this way he can then cover the material again if the students struggled to respond with the correct answers.

10. **Improvements and updates are a constant.** This is by far one of the best Google Classroom outlets for me. If something needs to be added or fixed, Google really listens and responds. This also means that teachers will have to keep learning while using it ... which is not bad either!

I'm sure there are more benefits to Google Classroom, but these are ten great reasons why it's worth taking a closer look.

50 Things You Can Do With Google Classroom

1. Make Class Announcements
2. Sharing Resources
3. Multiple Files in an Assignment
4. Create a Lesson
5. Easily View Student Submission
6. Go Paperless
7. Simplify the Turn In Process
8. Protect Privacy
9. Reduce Cheating
10. Classroom Collaboration
11. Create a Discussion
12. Organize Assignments with Due Dates
13. Feedback Before Students Submit
14. Email Students
15. Notify Students Who May Need Help
16. Assignment Q&A
17. Create an Ad Hoc Playlist
18. Email Feedback
19. Create Folders
20. Link Directly to Student Work
21. Collect Data
22. Share with Multiple Classes

23. Collaborative Note Taking
24. Display Student Work
25. One Student One Slide
26. Target Parent Phone Calls
27. Polling
28. Share a Document with the Class
29. Know Who Edits a Collaborative Document
30. Link to a Website
31. After Hours Help
32. Peer Feedback
33. Distribute Notes
34. Sharing Informal Learning
35. Email the Teacher
36. Student Projects
37. Eliminate Schlepping Papers Home
38. Have One Place for All Files
39. Document Digital Work
40. Students Create Google Docs
41. Clearly Identify Student Work
42. View Assignments
43. Virtual Office Hours
44. Collaborate with Peers (PLC's)
45. Virtual Faculty Meetings
46. Streamline Counseling
47. Watch Students Do Homework
48. Observe Another Classroom

49. Share Student Samples
50. Provide Choices

Advantages And Limitations Of Google Classroom

Benefits/ Advantages of Google Chrome & Google Classroom

1. **Unique view of student work:** To help educators track individual student progress, we have created a page in Classroom dedicated to each student that shows all of their work in a class. With this new view, teachers and students can view the status of each assignment and use filters to view assigned, missing, or returned and graded assignments. Teachers and students can use this information to make personalized learning decisions that help students set goals and develop skills that will serve them in the future.

2. **Rearrange Classes:** Teachers can now order their classes based on daily schedule, workload priorities, or whatever helps them stay organized throughout the school year. And students can also use this function. "For teachers and students, organization is important, and being able to rearrange class cards allows us to keep our classes organized in a simple and personalized way," says Ross Berman, 7th and 8th grade math teacher. "Students can move classes so that the first thing they see is the class they know

they will have work to do."

3. **Decimal grading :** As teachers know, grading is often more complicated than a simple point value. To be as accurate as possible with their assessment, educators can now use decimal points when grading assignments in Google Classroom.

4. **Transfer ownership of the class:** Things can change a lot during the summer, including who is teaching what class. Administrators and teachers can now transfer ownership of classes in Google Classroom to other teachers, without having to redo the class. The new class owner can quickly catch up on a full view of the work and resources of past students on Drive.

5. **Add a profile picture from a mobile device:** Students today accumulate many hours of use on their phones. Soon, students will be able to make changes to their mobile profile in Classroom directly from their mobile devices, including changing their profile picture from the Google Classroom mobile app. Get the selfies ready!

6. **Manage classes with School Directory Sync:** Google School Directory Sync now supports synchronization of Google Classroom classes from your student information management system using IMS OneRoster CSV files . Administrators can save teachers and students time by managing class setup before the start of school bell rings.

7. **New Classroom Integrations:** The apps that integrate with Classroom provide a seamless experience for educators and allow them to easily share information between Classroom and other tools they like.Welcome new apps to the #withClassroom family : Quizizz , Edcite , Kami, and coming soon, Code.org .

8. **Show the class code:** Joining Google Classroom classes is easier than ever thanks to this new update. Teachers can now display their class code in full screen so students can quickly join new classes.

9. **A preview! Import self-assessment test scores on Google Forms into Classroom:** Using self-assessment tests on Google Forms allows educators to assess students' understanding of a topic in real time. Soon, teachers will be able to import test scores directly into Google Classroom.

10. **Add comments to the test question-by-question score:** Beyond **test** scores, meaningful feedback can improve learning.

Advantages

Its operation is very simple and intuitive , and in fact this is the key to its success. It is not as comprehensive as other learning platforms, but any teacher uses it with ease with minimal training. In fact, all online communication with students is done with this tool. It is no longer necessary to use email, much less WhatsApp or insecure user applications. Thus, the teacher can send notifications to his class (or to a specific group) replacing the paper "agenda", and allowing the children to interact.

It also allows you **to ask follow-up questions**, with the advantage of having instantly the individual answers of each student, and also the general result. And of course, it also **offers the possibility of sending tasks** and thus avoid making photocopies for everyone. With a simple click, each one has their copy of the work, to carry it out, from anywhere (school, home), at any time, and from any device (mobile, tablet , laptop or pc of any brand and model).

In general, it **saves administrative paperwork** and allows a better organization in addition to working with text, videos, images, equations, mind maps, staves, and any product that can be created digitally.

Disadvantages/ Limitations

There is really no pressing challenge with the Google Classroom. In return, it **requires that each teacher and student have a "Google" account** , which causes some families some concern , in my opinion unfounded because for educational accounts Google's privacy conditions are very strict.

CHAPTER 8: GOOGLE CLASSROOM TIPS AND TRICKS

3 Tips to Organize Your Google Classroom -

In this section, we're going to have a look at how to keep your Google Classroom nice and organized. There are three basic strategies that we can use to ensure that our Google Classroom doesn't get messy. And they are:

1. Organizing by topics,
2. Reusing posts, and;
3. Archiving and deleting classrooms that we don’t know longer need.

Why don't we look at each of these strategies one at a time. And we are going to start with topics.

1. Topics

Topics are probably the easiest way to make sure that the content that you post on the Google Classroom doesn't get out of hand and it's easily accessible by you and your students. To use topics to organize your Google classroom, go to classwork, click Create and click on the topic.

Before you create any topics, think about how you would like to compartmentalize everything that you've posted on your Google Classroom. You might have a bunch of assignments, batch of questions, bunch of materials and so forth. Think about what are the topics that all your posts can fall into. Tutors normally compartmentalize their content by either units or type of posts.

So let me demonstrate first, how can we categorize our post by units. So to do that, we're going to create three units that I'm teaching this semester. We're going to create unit one, create another unit, Unit Two, and unit three. You might have noticed that once I've created those units, they appear on the left of my screen as a table of content because I have some posts that have been generated before I can now try and sort them out. So I know that assignment one belongs to unit one. So what I will do I will simply take it and drag it to unit one. Immediately, assignment one will disappear from my posts he up top and will show up under unit one. I will do the same for other posts. My first quiz assignment belongs to unit three. My question about creativity belongs to Unit Two. My essay prompts belong to unit three and out my assignment two belongs to Unit Two. I think we started to see how our Google Classroom can look much more organized.

When we start using topics, there are a couple of things you can do when it comes to editing the topics. First thing is renaming. Once you've set up a name, you can rename it later on, you can move them up and down or dragging them from the old topics view. One important thing to remember why delete into topic is that when you delete a topic, the posts that belong to this topic won't be deleted. What I've done right now I've deleted unit three, which had essay prompts and my first quiz assignment, but they're, they've just been moved up to an unassigned topic. So this is one way to organize all of your content organizing by units.

What you can also do is organize all your content according to the type of the post Google Classroom allows you to create four different types assignment quiz, assignment questions and materials. And this could be your topics. So why don't we go ahead and try and organize in this way, our first topic is going to be assignment. Our second topic is going to be quiz assignment. Our third topic is going to be question. And finally, our fourth topic is going to be material assignment. We'll go on to the assignment material, we'll go on to the material and so forth. There's one more thing I need to point out is that you can assign your posts to topics while you're creating them to do that, while you're creating, let's say a question right here you can select to which topic this particular post will be assigned to. This is a question I posed. So this will be assigned to a question once I post this question, it will automatically go on to the question topic. This is just two ways to categorize your posts. You can come up with your own method, but this is what I personally do either organizing by units or type of assignments.

2. Reuse Posts

Another thing you can do to help you keep your Google Classroom organized, is to reuse posts. I think it's easier to demonstrate how it's done. So let's say this is my second Google classroom that doesn't have anything and classwork. So instead of creating an assignment from scratch, what I can do is I can reuse posts generated in another Google Classroom. Let me demonstrate what I mean. If I go to create and click reuse posts, we use post with first asked me, okay, which class would I would like to use a post from this is the second Google classroom and I would like to reuse posts from my first Google Classroom. So this will take me to my first Google classroom, and I can select a post that I would like to reuse in my second Google Classroom. So in my case, I would like to reuse assignment. One, make sure when you use policy Create new copies for all attachments so that attachments are not shared between two groups of students. When I click reuse now assignment, one that was originally generated and my first Google Classroom appeared in my second Google classroom, so this is a really nice way to keep it organized. Instead of creating a new post over and over again, reuse post function enables you to recycled posts that have been generated before for the current classrooms.

3. Archiving And Deleting Classrooms

Our final strategy to help you keep your Google Classroom neat and organized is archiving and deleting classrooms that you no longer teach. By the end of the school year, a lot of teachers approached me with the same question how do we delete Google classrooms that we don't no longer teach? We taught them last year. Now we have another group of students, and we don't need Google classrooms from last year. And you will be surprised that it's not a straightforward process. And there's a reason behind that.

So how do we delete Google Classroom we no longer need. To live in a classroom and Google Classroom requires two steps. When you open a Google Classroom, make sure you go to classes and you see all classes. I want to delete my second Google Classroom. I taught a group of students this year, and now not gonna teach in that next year and I want to delete this class. Now if you click on three dots in the top right corner, you won't see delete option and this is where people normally go to edit or delete, but delete is no longer there. Because Google Classroom is set up in such a way is that before you delete, you need to archive it. Google Classroom will warn you that students won't be able to access this class but it will appear in archived classes. Now when it's been archived, when we can finally delete it. Click on three lines in the top left corner and scroll all the way down to archived classes. You will see the class that has been archived at. Now when you click on three dots, you will see an option to delete. And this is how you delete your class permanently.

So you might be wondering, why is that I need to archive first and then delete it. And this is the answer. When the class is archived, there are two things you can do. First, you can always restore this class. If I click Restore, it will be moved back, and students will be able to access that.

Another thing you can do with archive classes, you can reuse posts made in this class before. So let's imagine that I still teach my first Google classroom and I want to reuse some posts that were made in my second Google classroom and the second Google classroom has been archived. I don't see it in my homescreen but it can still source or take some materials from there. If I go to classwork in my first google classroom, click Create and click 'reuse posts'. You will notice that in this selector of the classes, I can still see my second group Little classroom, even though I don't see it on my home screen, where I normally see my classes, I can see once I start, we use post, but it is marked that it has been archived, I can select my second Google classroom, and I can use some posts that are there. And that's the main difference between deleting an archive.

So, on a final note, we've looked at how to keep our Google Classroom nice and organized. Let's look at how we can use topics to compartmentalize the posts that we've created. We looked at how we can reuse posts that were made previously. We also look at how to archive classes How to delete a class, so it's no longer visible in either a home screen or an archived classes.

CONCLUSION

This platform is presented as a great tool to increase interaction in classes , decrease paper consumption and reduce costs in schools and universities.

One of the main benefits of this platform is that it can be used very well in Blended learning, which is a mix between e-learning and conventional learning.

I highly recommend this tool for educational institutions that are thinking of migrating your processes to the digital way (E-learning), using this platform in conjunction with face-to-face classes (Mixed Learning), can help us make a progressive and friendly migration.

Regarding the sale of courses on the Internet or the training of personnel, you will not have any chance to use this infrastructure, since it does not offer any information security protocol, which can be a problem in terms of content privacy.

As you can see, in this book l have shared with you how I use it, how I create the classes, I invite the students, how I assign the tasks or how to notify them on the class board. All this now, will make us be closer than ever with our students.

I hope this guide on How to use Google Classroom inside and outside the classroom is helpful.

Good luck!

APPRECIATION

We sincerely appreciate your purchase of our eBook that reveals useful information about everything you need to know about the Google Classroom. We hope you love it.

Thanks

Anna Smith.

GOOGLE CLASSROOM

(Aulas de Google)

La guía completa de 2020 para estudiantes y profesores sobre cómo beneficiarse del aprendizaje a distancia y configurar su aula virtual

Por

© Anna Smith and Carlos Moya

PUBLICADO POR: © **Anna Smith and Carlos Moya**

ISBN:

TABLE OF CONTENTS

INTRODUCTION 1

CAPÍTULO 1: ¿QUÉ ES GOOGLE CLASSROOM? 3

Google Classroom: La escuela en tiempo de coronavirus 3

Como configurar Google Classroom en tres pasos 12

Beneficios de Google Classroom para los profesores 15

Las ventajas de Google Classroom en el curso de las clases 17

Beneficios de Google Classroom para estudiantes 18

CAPÍTULO 2: APRENDIZAJE ACTIVO Y ESCUELA EN CASA 20

Interacción de Classroom: ¿Cómo ayuda Google Classroom? . 20

Elementos involucrados en la enseñanza-aprendizaje en linea 24

Entonces, ¿cuál debería elegir? 45

Educación virtual: ventajas, mitos y consejos para mejorar los resultados 49

Mito 1. La calidad de la educación virtual es inferior 51

Mito 2. Los maestros no están capacitados para enseñar en línea 52

Mito 3. La educación virtual es una moda 52

Consejos para afrontar con éxito el reto de la educación virtual 54

CAPÍTULO 3: VISIÓN DEL PROFESOR 56
AULA DE GOOGLE PARA PROFESORES 56
Cómo crear y recopilar tareas de los estudiantes 61
Cómo utilizar las rúbricas 71
CAPÍTULO 4: VISTA DEL ESTUDIANTE 75
Google Classroom para estudiantes: acceso a Google Classroom 75
DESDE UN DISPOSITIVO MÓVIL 80
Guía básica de Google Aula para estudiantes 81
AULA DE GOOGLE PARA ESTUDIANTES 83
CAPÍTULO 5: EXTENSIÓN Y APLICACIONES 90
Las 13 mejores extensiones de Google Chrome imprescindibles para profesores 90
Las 12 mejores aplicaciones de Google Classroom 99
CAPÍTULO 6: OTRAS COSAS INCREÍBLES SOBRE EL AULA DE GOOGLE 104
Diez razones por las que debería utilizar Google Classroom. 104
50 cosas que puedes hacer con Google Classroom 108
Ventajas y limitaciones de Google Classroom 111
CAPÍTULO 7: CONSEJOS Y TRUCOS PARA EL AULA DE GOOGLE 116
Tres consejos para organizar tu clase de Google: 116
CONCLUSIÓN 123
APRECIACIÓN 125

INTRODUCTION

Un número cada vez mayor de profesores está utilizando la plataforma Google Classroom, que permite centrarse menos en la tecnología y más en la enseñanza, ya que permite organizar un aula virtual y lecciones a distancia sin ser necesariamente un profesional de la tecnología.

En este libro, veremos todo lo que necesita para comenzar con Google Classroom y lo que te permite hacer. A continuación, veremos cómo configurar una clase y crear trabajos como asignaciones, asignaciones de cuestionarios, preguntas y proporcionar materiales didácticos. Saltemos de inmediato.

Un incremento en número de profesores que usan la plataforma Google Classroom (salón de clases de Google), el cual te permite enfocarte menos en la tecnologia y más en la enseñanza, asi también te permite organizar aulas virtuales y lecciones a distancia sin la necesidad de ser un profesional con la tecnología.

En este libro te mostraremos lo que necesitas para comenzar con *Google Classroom* y con lo que este te permite hacer. Posteriormente, te enseñaremos a como crear tareas como asignaturas, cuestionarios, encuestas y, proveer materiales de enseñanza. ¡Demos un paso adelante!

CAPÍTULO 1:
¿QUÉ ES GOOGLE CLASSROOM?

Google Classroom: La escuela en tiempo de coronavirus

El programa de aprendizaje a distancia de Google se ha convertido en uno de los más ampliamente usados e interesantes globalmente.

El coronavirus cambió la vida de muchos de nosotros, pero mayormente la vida de los niños y adolescentes. De hecho, durante meses las escuelas están cerradas, las reglas han cambiado y así también la enseñanza y con ello todas las dificultades puesto que han sido cambiadas a los hogares de los niños y profesores filtrados a través de las pantallas de sus computadoras y la conexión de internet.

Esta es una forma—aunque no completamente nueva— de aprender y enseñar, pero inesperadamente se está volviendo central en los últimos tiempos. Por lo tanto, la herramienta del momento solo podría ser Google Classroom, el conjunto de programas y servicios diseñados por Mountain View para unir a profesores y estudiantes. ¿El programa reemplaza las lecciones de clase dignamente?

Lo que es

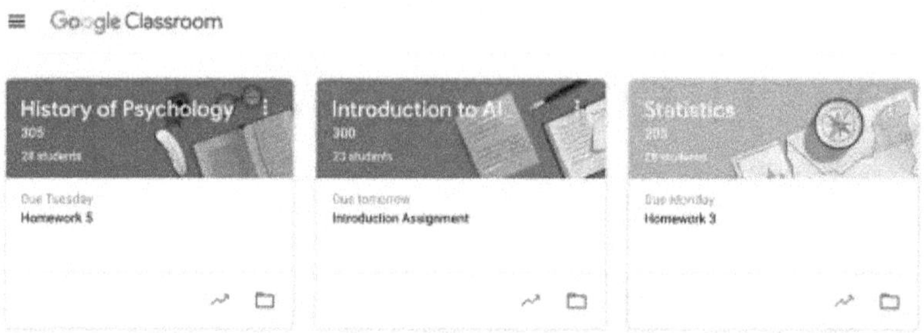

Google Classroom no es más que un programa que facilita el aprendizaje a distancia al ofrecer una serie de posibilidades para compartir y una sinergia total con las funciones clásicas del mundo de Google. Está disponible de forma gratuita durante seis años y ya ampliamente utilizado por muchos educadores, el programa se ha convertido en el más utilizado por los maestros y profesores en estos tiempos de pandemia. Sus funciones te permiten asignar ejercicios, pruebas y cuestionarios, almacenar material didáctico en un espacio compartido, compartir videos e intercambiar mensajes rápidamente.

Un código único es suficiente para que los alumnos de tu clase creen un "ambiente privado" bastante similar al de las paredes de la escuela, accesible solo para el maestro que creó la sala y para los alumnos a quienes se envió el código.

Con una cuenta de Google en unos pocos minutos de configuración, puedes aprovechar el servicio, accesible desde una PC o teléfono inteligente a través de una aplicación. En el interior, los estudiantes pueden verificar los plazos de tareas, actualizarse cuando llegue nuevo contenido y recibir calificaciones. Máximiza también la posibilidad de comunicación, tanto entre alumnos como con el profesor, inevitable la posibilidad de realizar video lecciones.

Seis años de historia

Google Classroom anunció y presentó una vista previa para determinados usuarios el 6 de mayo de 2014, se diseñó inicialmente para miembros del programa *G Suite for Education*. Inicialmente, incluso después del lanzamiento oficial, la aplicación estaba vinculada a miembros pagos de

G Suite. Una estrategia que duró más o menos tres años: en marzo de 2017, el servicio estaba abierto a cualquier usuario con una cuenta de Google, y también brindaba a los miembros que no pertenecían a G Suite la oportunidad de participar en lecciones o crear nuevas.

En 2018 se lanzó una importante actualización del programa, con nuevas secciones de trabajo, una interfaz de evaluación mejorada y nuevas funciones para estudiantes y maestros. 'Today Classroom', además de sus 78 temas ilustrados, ofrece compatibilidad total con Google Drive para archivar y enviar documentos, con Gmail para comunicaciones, con Calendar para administrar plazos y avisos y con varios programas de administración y creación de archivos como Google Docs, Sheets y Presentaciones.

Más recientemente surgió la compatibilidad total con Hangout para gestionar una comunicación más inmediata entre los componentes de una clase y dar vida a las sesiones de video real.

Facilidad de entrada

Ciertamente, la difusión de Classroom se favoreció por la innegable facilidad de uso de sus servicios y por su grado de familiaridad con los hábitos de los usuarios. Tener una cuenta de Google significa conocer ya muchos de los servicios que son la base del funcionamiento de su programa escolar; el punto fuerte de la aplicación es, de hecho, su **muy fuerte sinergia con la galaxia de Google**, perfectamente integrada en ella. Drive se usa para almacenar documentos y lecciones, Hangouts para video lecciones o chats, todo sin tener que pagar absolutamente nada, con la máxima compatibilidad con muchas aplicaciones y sin algun tipo de publicidad.

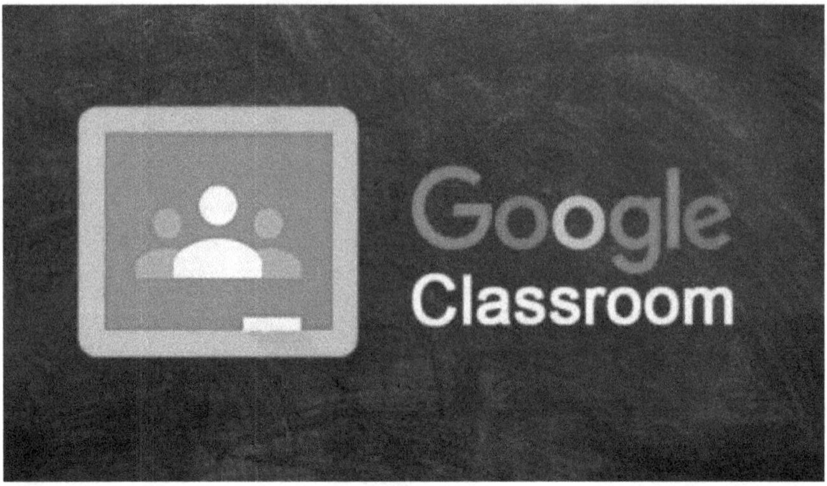

Un servicio diferenciadoen el entorno entre profesores y alumnos, pero que comparte las mismas herramientas de trabajo con la máxima compatibilidad. Básicamente, basta con tener un mínimo de familiaridad con los distintos programas de la suite de Google para poder utilizar todo con la máxima eficacia. Una sencillez de propósito que había llevado a Classroom al centro de la escena incluso en tiempos insospechados y que ahora ha hecho imprescindible continuar con la labor educativa en tiempos de encierro.

Maestros, estudiantes y padres

Los profesores representan el centro neurálgico de Classroom: desde su página pueden gestionar las distintas clases que han creado, con la posibilidad de compartir materiales, asignar tareas y comprobar el progreso de cada trabajo asignado a sus alumnos. A través del calendario puedes gestionar citas o plazos y organizar reuniones de grupo. **Los alumnos**, por su parte, además de participar en actividades colectivas, tienen numerosas posibilidades para completar las tareas que se les asignen. Estos se pueden gestionar de forma rápida e intuitiva, con la capacidad de elegir qué aplicación utilizar para completar el trabajo según la solicitud de tu profesor.

Una vez completado, todo se puede cargar y será visto por el profesor, quien tendrá el control total de todos los trabajos y los plazos correspondientes. También es interesante la **posibilidad de que los padres de familia puedan monitorear la clase de** sus hijos a través de la función, siempre filtrada por los profesores, para tener acceso a un sistema de correo electrónico en el que estar actualizado sobre el progreso del trabajo, las lecciones que se imparten e información más general sobre el tema progreso de la clase. En definitiva, un microcosmos escolar en todos los aspectos.

El sistema de evaluacion

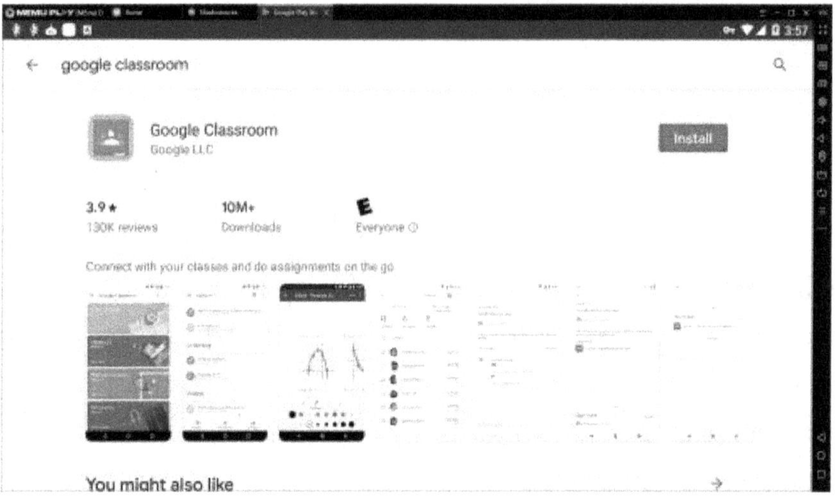

Una de las funciones más apreciadas de Classroom es, sin duda alguna, la de evaluación, con **la posibilidad de que los profesores retroalimenten el trabajo realizado por los alumnos.** Los esquemas de votación son numerosos, con opciones para adjuntar archivos a las asignaciones, posibilidad de monitorear el progreso de cada alumno, además de realizar comentarios, cambios o anotaciones en tiempo real. Una vez finalizado y enviado su trabajo, los profesores tienen la posibilidad de devolverlo con notas y correcciones que a su vez permiten a los propios alumnos corregir los errores cometidos.

Además, es un sistema de evaluación y corrección en tiempo real que permite seguir paso a paso el procedimiento de todo lo que desees, corrigiendo errores de raíz y con posibilidad de interacción durante la realización de actividades que son difíciles de replicar en condiciones normales o con las tradicionales métodos. Una posibilidad de no poca importancia y ciertamente un aspecto positivo en una situación de emergencia como esta y que, si se desarrolla adecuadamente, **podría hacer de Classroom una herramienta muy útil también junto a la enseñanza más tradicional.**

Una escuela a distancia para todos

A lo largo de los años, sin embargo, se han realizado muchas críticas hacia Classroom, comenzando por la falta de apertura a servicios o archivos externos a las herramientas proporcionadas por Google y a un número limitado de herramientas de verificación como cuestionarios o pruebas automáticas. También ha habido acusaciones en la gestión no exactamente transparente de los datos de los usuarios, lo cual es muy valioso ya que casi siempre se trata de menores o niños.

Google siempre ha reiterado su atención a la privacidad, peroel **almacenamiento y el archivo de los datos de los estudiantes sigue siendo uno de los temas más candentes que giran en torno al programa.** A pesar de ello, la gran utilidad del servicio para alumnos y profesores es innegable; Es fundamental, de hecho, que la enseñanza continúe a toda costa y que la educación no se detenga ni siquiera en condiciones como estas.

Por lo tanto, todos los programas que ayudan a la educación a distancia son por tanto fundamentales, más aún si se integran con aplicaciones que muchos de nosotros ya utilizamos a diario como las de Google. Será fundamental que estas herramientas se utilicen cada vez más, incluso en condiciones normales, porque son útiles para mejorar una enseñanza y una escuela ancladas con demasiada frecuencia al pasado. Al mismo tiempo, será **fundamental proteger a todas las partes involucradas y garantizar que estos instrumentos no se conviertan en discriminadores o amplificadores de diferencias.**

De hecho, no todo el mundotiene la posibilidad de acceder a ciertas herramientas o de conexiones rápidas que les permitan usarlas y no todos son capaces de comprender mejor todas las funciones. Dar acceso y uso equitativo a todos será esencial para que un modelo de enseñanza en línea funcione y sea sostenible en el futuro. Tener la mejor de las herramientas en sus manos es inútil si no se puede utilizar de la mejor manera posible. Y esto, en un mundo delicado como el de la educación y la escuela, nunca debemos olvidarlo.

Como configurar Google Classroom en tres pasos

1. **Inicia sesión** con tu cuenta de la escuela o un Gmail normal. Cuando vayas a **classroom.google.com** puedes utilizar la sala de clase por el acceso utilizando una dirección de correo electrónico G suite o puede utilizar una cuenta de Gmail normal.

2. **Crea tu primera lección.** Haz clic en el botón "+" en la esquina superior derecha. Elige "crear curso". Allí, ingresa información detallada sobre tu clase. El nombre de la clase será el título de la clase para que pueda encontrarla en segundos. Luego, haz clic en "crear".

3. **Invita a los estudiantes a tu clase.** Una vez que hayas creado el curso, verás bajo el título el código que se utilizará para invitar a tus alumnos. Vé al menú Personas y desde allí comienza a invitar a tus estudiantes ingresando un nombre o dirección de correo electrónico.

¡Ahora tu curso en línea está listo! Al menos, está ahí y todos pueden acceder a el. Hay algunas otras cosas que debe hacer antes de tomarse en serio.

Crear y asignar una oferta en tu Curso

Para **crear tareas para asignar a tu clase** en el menú superior, vaya a "Trabajo del curso" y haz clic en "+ Crear", se abrirá una ventana desplegable que propondrá los posibles trabajos que puedes crear.

Por ejemplo, al elegir "Tarea con Quiz" se abrirá un panel donde podrás configurar el trabajo a asignar, solo tendrás que ingresar el Título, si quieres las instrucciones y pulsar en "Test en blanco" el cual ingresa a las preguntas, múltiples respuestas y la calificación deseada.

Si deseas **agregar material para compartir,** todo lo que tiene que hacer es hacer clic en "+ Crear" y seleccionar "Material", asignar un título y una descripción y agregar un archivo en Google Drive, un enlace, un archivo en tu computadora o un video YouTube.

Por supuesto, hay mucho más que decir sobre Google Classroom, lo que acabamos de enfrentar es el camino básico que aún te permitirá crear una clase y asignar tareas a los alumnos.

Beneficios de Google Classroom para los profesores

La nueva plataforma de Google está diseñada para mejorar la relación entre estudiantes y profesores. Google Classroom facilita la interacción en las clases.

Google ha lanzado su nueva plataforma para mejorar la interacción con los estudiantes en clase:

- Compartir documentos con tus alumnos y notificarles la convocatoria del examen se puede hacer de forma inmediata gracias a la nueva plataforma de Google.
- Los estudiantes ahora pueden entregar su trabajo en formato digital en línea gracias a Google Classroom. Esta plataforma mejora la comunicación profesor-alumno.
- Google Classroom ayuda a mejorar la interacción con los estudiantes, haciendo que las clases sean más fluidas.

Google ha lanzado su nueva plataforma para mejorar la interacción con los estudiantes en clase. **Google Classroom** mantiene a los estudiantes y al profesor en contacto.

Internet facilita la vida de las personas en diferentes áreas. Gracias a **Google Classroom** es más fácil seguir las clases y compartir el material con los alumnos. Esta plataforma en línea está diseñada para mejorar la comunicación y el flujo de trabajo entre alumno y profesor.

El acceso a Google Classroom solo requiere una cuenta de Google y una **conexión a Internet**. La plataforma funciona como una red social diseñada para facilitar los temas tratados en clase.

Conseguir el material necesario para **seguir las clases** a los alumnos suele ser complicado para los profesores. Google Classroom ha desarrollado una nueva solución. Esta plataforma te permite compartir documentos y crear un calendario donde los estudiantes pueden conocer las fechas de los exámenes y la entrega de trabajos.

El aula es **un espacio de convivencia**. Internet permite ampliar este espacio después del horario escolar. La plataforma diseñada por Google permite a los alumnos acceder a toda la información de la clase online, para que puedan repasar la asignatura y ponerse al día, en el caso de que hayan estado enfermos y no hayan ido a clase.

Las ventajas de Google Classroom en el curso de las clases

1. Comparta el calendario de los exámenes y las asignaciones de trabajo con los estudiantes.

Google Classroom permite compartir información relevante sobre el curso de la asignatura con los estudiantes. De esta manera, pueden averiguar fácilmente cuándo hay un examen o cuándo deben presentar un trabajo.

2. Facilitar la entrega de trabajos de clase en formato digital

La entrega de trabajos gracias a Google Classroom se puede realizar online. De esta formano hay necesidad de imprimir los trabajos y hacer tal desperdicio de papel. Por ello, esta aplicación facilita la entrega digital de trabajos de clase.

3. Envío de material extra para preparar las clases

Muchos profesores piden a sus alumnos que hagan lecturas antes de que comiencen las clases. La plataforma de Google permite compartir estos textos con los alumnos de forma rápida y cómoda.

4. Informar al alumno de las novedades cuando no pueda acudir al aula.

Para actualizar a un estudiante que no ha podido asistir a clase, Google Classroom es perfecto. El alumno enfermo puede estar en contacto con las clases del profesor a través de Internet.

Beneficios de Google Classroom para estudiantes

Responsivo

Google Classroom se puede ejecutar en todos los dispositivos sin ningún problema, ya sea un teléfono o Android, tableta o PC.

Fomentar la comunicación y el trabajo colaborativo

Al ser un producto de google, esta plataforma está **integrada con Google Doc**, por lo que **permite la creación de documentos, tablas y presentaciones de manera conjunta entre los estudiantes**, esta puede ser una herramienta para promover el trabajo en grupo y el uso de herramientas digitales.

Dejar la tarea y las asignaciones se vuelve más fácil

Gracias a Google Clasrroom, dejar una tarea o asignatura se puede simplificar a 1 clic, por lo que puedes enviar el tiempo para imprimir material, distribuirlo, y luego recopilarlo y clasificarlo, esto es un gran alivio tanto para el profesor como para los alumnos.

Adios a los papeles

El cuidado del medio ambiente es un tema cada vez más relevante, solo uno de los principales objetivos de esta plataforma es ahorrar papel, evitar imprimir lecturas, formatos y material educativo, y compartirlo todo con un solo clic.

Uso amigable

Google en el aula es muy fácil de usar, por lo que no nee z d para pasar horas aprendiendo a usar esta plataforma, sólo se tarda unos 15 minutos para entender cómo funcionan las características más básicas.

Tiene una integración con Google Suite

Al ser un producto de Google, Classroom está integrado con toda la suite de Google para que pueda compartir información de las siguientes aplicaciones:

- Google Drive
- calendario de Google
- Hojas de cálculo de Google
- Youtube
- Formularios de Google

CAPÍTULO 2:
APRENDIZAJE ACTIVO Y ESCUELA EN CASA

Interacción de Classroom: ¿Cómo ayuda Google Classroom?

Hay un cambio notable en las prácticas educativas, principalmente para integrar cada vez más la tecnología de una manera que sea beneficiosa para profesores y alumnos. Google Classroom, una aplicación que forma parte de Google for Education, es una de esas herramientas que ayudan a agilizar el proceso de enseñanza-aprendizaje.

Usualmente conocido por facilitar la comunicación entre la clase. La aplicación tiene muchas otras funciones que merecen ser exploradas. Y, contrariamente a la creencia popular, también es muy útil en cursos presenciales y no solo en educación a distancia.

¿Eres nuevo en Classroom todavía? ¿Se pregunta cómo puede hacer que su graduación sea mucho más interactiva y rentable? ¡Así que sigue leyendo esta publicación para responder estas y otras preguntas!

¿Que es Google Classroom?

En 2014, «**Google for Education**» (Google para la education) llegó a Brasil con la promesa de aportar una perspectiva completamente nueva sobre la integración entre tecnología y educación. La propuesta de la reconocida multinacional es ofrecer recursos a instituciones, docentes y estudiantes para agilizar el proceso de enseñanza-aprendizaje y actualizar las prácticas educativas.

G Suite for Education, por ejemplo, está disponible de forma gratuita e integra el acceso a correo electrónico institucional, almacenamiento ilimitado en Google Drive, Calendar, Google Sheets, Forms y Slides. Otra herramienta importante de 'Google for Education' es Google Classroom, un espejo de aula en línea que proporciona más intercambio entre estudiantes y profesores.

Esta aplicación es un claro ejemplo de que la tecnología no está separada de la educación, pero es de gran ayuda cuando se utiliza correctamente.

Google Classroom es una herramienta de gestión, organización y colaboración que hace que el aprendizaje sea mucho más productivo. A través de la plataforma es posible enviar trabajos, recibir calificaciones, responder preguntas con profesores y compañeros y mucho más.

La práctica interfaz de la aplicación permite que incluso aquellos que no están muy familiarizados con otros recursos tecnológicos la utilicen sin dificultad. El objetivo es hacer más atractiva la dinámica de las clases y, al mismo tiempo, más accesible.

Aula digital en la práctica

Pero, ¿cómo funciona todo, en términos prácticos? Cada estudiante de la institución debe registrarse utilizando un correo electrónico institucional específico para tal fin, el cual es puesto a disposición por la institución. Posteriormente, el profesor es responsable de conectar a todos sus alumnos en una clase en línea a través del Classroom.

A partir de ahí, estarán disponibles las infinitas posibilidades de la aplicación, que pueden y deben utilizarse. Para el docente, la herramienta ayuda en la gestión de las clases y en la facilidad para abordar cuestiones administrativas, verificar calificaciones, transmitir anuncios e insertar evaluaciones en el sistema.

Los estudiantes también se benefician de la herramienta, lo que permite enviar sus trabajos y actividades con mucha más facilidad. Pero la interacción proporcionada por Classroom va mucho más allá y puede "salvar" la experiencia de pregrado para los estudiantes.

La falta de actualización de los métodos de enseñanza y el seguimiento individualizado de los estudiantes se consideran dos de las principales razones que conducen a la deserción escolar en la educación superior. Según una investigación publicada en 2007 por el Journal of College Student Retention, las innovaciones en el proceso de enseñanza y una mayor comunicación entre profesores y alumnos son estímulos fundamentales que llevan a la conclusión del curso.

Ésta, de hecho, es la principal propuesta de la herramienta; puede usarse en cualquier momento, promueve la comunicación instantánea y sirve casi como una red social educativa.

Los miembros de la clase pueden publicar enlaces, comentarios y hacer preguntas, teniendo la oportunidad de proyectar su voz sin el tiempo y el espacio limitados que ocurre en un aula convencional.

Los maestros también pueden monitorear el progreso de cada estudiante en las actividades, verificando dónde necesitan más apoyo e intervención. Aún queda espacio para que la valoración se haga en detalle, ya que el medio digital garantiza esta flexibilidad.

En línea y fuera de línea

En el caso de una universidad a distancia, la comunicación e interacción constantes son fundamentales e incluso definen la calidad del curso ofrecido. Como los cursos de educación a distancia no tienen el factor de presencia, deben abusar de toda la tecnología disponible para estimular el aprendizaje.

El Aula garantiza fluidez en la logística y un sentimiento de cercanía con el docente, requisitos importantes para que el alumno no se sienta solo en este recorrido.

Para una graduación presencial, la nueva dinámica hace que las clases sean más estimulantes, fomenta la participación de todos los estudiantes y además de eso permite que el proceso de aprendizaje sea mucho más activo.

Todavía existe la posibilidad de conectar Classroom con otras aplicaciones y mejorar su funcionalidad. Herramientas como Classcraft y Quizizz convierten las actividades regulares en misiones o cuestionarios, haciendo que cualquier trabajo sea mucho más divertido, sin perder el enfoque ni la calidad.

Continúa nuestra sección sobre herramientas de Google para una enseñanza sencilla, dinámica e inclusiva.

Google ofrece herramientas gratuitas que son útiles tanto para profesores como para estudiantes. Se acabaron los largos cursos de formación para la gestión externa que necesitan actualizaciones constantes y son difíciles de utilizar o superfluos en la vida diaria.

Elementos involucrados en la enseñanza-aprendizaje en linea

Enseñando y aprendiendo

Enseñar y aprender desde la virtualidad hoy requiere docentes capaces de transformar su práctica pedagógica utilizando las nuevas tecnologías de la información y la comunicación (TIC) para servir a sus alumnos y enfrentar los desafíos culturales y técnicos que conducen a un cambio dinámico y complejo sobre qué, cómo y por qué enseñar.

Estas condiciones promueven un proceso de aprendizaje personalizado y colaborativo y una acción docente que busca satisfacer las necesidades e intereses de los estudiantes para el desarrollo de sus habilidades a través de la interacción con el contexto virtual. En este sentido, el propósito de este ensayo es reflexionar sobre el proceso de enseñanza y aprendizaje desde la virtualidad considerando los elementos teóricos educativos involucrados en este proceso. Para ello, se abordaron la educación virtual y sus elementos, el aprendizaje colaborativo, las estrategias de enseñanza virtual y las competencias docentes en esta modalidad educativa. Se espera que los docentes en su práctica promuevan una educación pedagógica transformadora que pueda despertar en el grupo de estudiantes la motivación para aprender de forma activa y acorde a los avances que presenta la sociedad.

Introducción

En la actualidad, el mundo se enfrenta a una serie de cambios históricos de carácter político, social, económico y tecnológico, que, si se sabe afrontarlos, se puede aprovechar al máximo para el bienestar y progreso de los pueblos; sin embargo, esto requiere tiempo para analizarlos, comprenderlos y tratarlos. La educación como un factor de desarrollo social no ha escapado a estos procesos, por lo que, según Tedesco (2009), es necesario para la educación de evolucionar y transformar de manera que esas naciones puedan asimilar estos cambios y el proceso junto a ellos, y no detrás.

Así, en referencia el autor afirma que la educación tradicional no está respondiendo a las demandas económicas actuals. Polanco (2011), afirma que esta educación, también denominada 'educación tradicional presencial', trata al alumno como un espectador, en la que el acto didáctico se convierte en ilusión; de ahí la urgencia de reformarlo y consolidar un nuevo compromiso educativo que propicie la formación de un individuo con mejores capacidades humanas, intelectuales y sociales, con interés en la experimentación, la creatividad, la autonomía en las decisiones, la responsabilidad y la cooperación en el trabajo que realizan.

Por otro lado, Salinas (2004) señala que, para adaptar y transformar esta realidad de la sociedad actual, lasInstituciones Educativas deben flexibilizarse y desarrollar formas de integración y enseñanza virtual que incluyan las TIC en los procesos de formación educativa. Desde el punto de vista de Barriga (2009) indica que las nuevas demandas dirigidas a la profesión docente exigen que los docentes sean responsables de la alfabetización tecnológica de sus alumnos y del dominio de una diversidad de competencias requeridas en el contexto de las demandas de la sociedad del conocimiento.

Como señala Lagos (2010), las TIC se han convertido en una herramienta indispensable para la mayoría de las actividades docentes; t oye ofrecen una variedad de recursos para utilizar en las aulas y enriquecer el proceso de enseñanza-aprendizaje. El mundo digital se incorpora gradualmente a las instituciones educativas, pero la tecnología por sí sola no mejora la calidad del proceso de enseñanza-aprendizaje; es necesario un cambio en la forma de enseñar y aprender porque si no, se caería en los mismos errores de la educación tradicional; por lo tanto, es importante conocer los elementos que permiten que la educación virtual se lleve a cabo de manera fructífera ; no se puede seguir enseñando a las generaciones futuras con los medios del pasado.

Las plataformas educativas virtuales son una herramienta que introduce al docente en la creación de cursos y talleres, de forma rápida y sencilla, que permiten gestionar y organizar contenidos a la medida del usuario. Como buenos ejemplos y entre los más conocidos están Dokeos y Moodle quehan desarrollado en torno al campo educativo y dan a este tipo de formación un gran interés pedagógico que genera una educación personalizada y una diversidad de cursos adaptados a todos los perfiles y demandas. La incorporación de estas plataformas en el ámbito educativo no solo debe centrarse en la inclusión de materiales educativos, sino también en el trabajo colaborativo que promueven estos entornos, así como en las habilidades didácticas que pueden generar con su aplicación. Estos espacios cuentan con diferentes tipos de herramientas: contenido, comunicación y evaluación y seguimiento. Todos ellos son esenciales para el aprendizaje educativo y didáctico de los estudiantes y permiten crear contenidos adaptados a objetivos, procedimientos y resultados definidos, así como colaborar con otros usuarios para ayudarnos a profundizar en el concepto de formación colectiva.

Elementos de la educación virtual

Camacho (2010) argumenta que la educación virtual aunque parezca contradictoria, sí permite el contacto personal entre el docente y el alumno: el intercambio de mensajes escritos y la posibilidad de un seguimiento detallado del progreso le otorga al docente un conocimiento del estudiantemucho mayor que en los cursos presenciales; la información también se puede adaptar a los usuarios debido a la modularidad del contenido. Por ende, para operar dentro de la educación virtual es fundamental conocer los elementos para impartir aprendizajes con el uso de la tecnología:

Exploración: el uso de internet o, más precisamente, la World Wide Web como herramienta de exploración abre las puertas de una fuente inagotable de información y recursos al docente y al alumno.

Experiencia: El alumno virtual se involucra en una nueva experiencia social y de aprendizaje que puede incluir la comunicación directa con su maestro, discusiones con sus compañeros o el estudio individual de los contenidos a su propio ritmo.

Compromiso: Los cursos virtuales ofrecen al alumno una oportunidad única de compartir experiencias con otros, reforzando el sentido de colaboración y comunidad. Además, el alumno recibe el control de su tiempo y recursos, y también, puede elegir el mejor camino de aprendizaje de acuerdo con sus preferencias y habilidades.

Flexibilidad: desde cualquier lugar y en cualquier momento, los estudiantes pueden acceder a sus cursos virtuales. Se estima que aproximadamente el 80% de las empresas ya han resuelto su acceso a internet, por lo que las barreras técnicas de acceso para los estudiantes trabajadores ya se han superado.

Noticias: los maestros tienen la oportunidad de actualizar sus materiales y temas de discusión al instante, manteniendo los cursos actualizados y consistentes con la actualidad. Esto supone que el docente, al utilizar las TIC como herramientas en el acto didáctico, se enfrenta a retos culturales y técnicos que conducen a un cambio dinámico y complejo sobre qué enseñar, cómo enseñar y por qué enseñar. Por ello, la educación virtual apoya la pedagogía a través de estrategias innovadoras para desarrollar el proceso de aprendizaje aliviando las grandes barreras y bloqueos cognitivos que surgen con la educación tradicional.

La enseñanza de un nd Estrategias de Aprendizaje i Educación n virtual

Esteban (2009) explica que las estrategias de enseñanza y aprendizaje utilizadas en la educación virtual generalmente se clasifican según actividades cognitivas. De acuerdo con este criterio, se clasifican desde las operaciones más básicas hasta las más elaboradas en asociativo, elaboración, organización y apoyo. Los asociativos son los más sencillos e involucran operaciones básicas que no promueven en sí mismas las relaciones entre conocimientos, pero pueden ser la base para su posterior elaboración, ya que aumentan la probabilidad de recordar literalmente la información sin introducir cambios estructurales en la misma. Un ejemplo en un aula virtual son los foros utilizados en el bloque 0, que contienen y dan a conocer al alumno toda la información del curso, los recursos.

Las estrategias de elaboración, según el autor en referencia, constituyen un paso intermedio entre las estrictamente asociativas, que no trabajan la información en sí, y las organizativas, que promueven nuevas estructuras de conocimiento. En la elaboración se pueden producir operaciones más sencillas en las que se establecen algunas relaciones, generalmente extrínsecas, entre elementos de la información que pueden servir de "andamiaje" para el aprendizaje a través de la elaboración de significados y otras, más complejas cuando la elaboración se da a partir de la significación. de los elementos de información. Un ejemplo de ellos es la sección de construcción que se ubica en el bloque académico del aula virtual; allí el alumno encuentra la verdad por sus propios medios y con el apoyo de sus compañeros; el tutor en esa sección no interactúa.

Las estrategias organizativas consisten en establecer, de manera explícita, relaciones internas entre los elementos que componen los materiales de aprendizaje y con los conocimientos previos que posee el sujeto; Un ejemplo de su uso en el aula virtual es la sección expositiva perteneciente al bloque académico, en la que se expone toda la información necesaria que el alumno debe conocer con la ayuda de videos, archivos, enlaces a páginas web, entre otros.

Finalmente, las estrategias de apoyo son aquellas que, según el autor citado, en lugar de ir a aprender los materiales, tienen la misión de incrementar la efectividad de ese aprendizaje mejorando las condiciones en las que ocurre; un ejemplo es la sección de rebote colocada en el bloque académico; su objetivo es que el aprendiz asimile y establezca relaciones entre lo que ya sabe y el nuevo aprendizaje presentado con la ayuda y colaboración de sus compañeros; Entre las actividades sugeridas se encuentran foros, wikis, chats, videoconferencias y blogs, en los que se comparte conocimiento y se generan confrontaciones sobre la información proporcionada por el tutor.

Estas concepciones de las diferentes estrategias nos llevan a reflexionar sobre el cómo, con qué y por qué enseñar en el acto educativo virtual, de tal forma que, para dar respuesta a estas preguntas y teniendo en cuenta la clasificación de las estrategias de los mencionados autor, se puede deducir que los elementos implícitos en cada uno de ellos serían los siguientes: en las estrategias de organización, el docente representa el establecimiento de la estructura necesaria para la sistematización racional del contenido, los recursos de interacción, los espacios de consulta y las actividades de interacción, a través de la determinación de jerarquías, ordenamiento, correlación y agrupamiento de actividades con el fin de realizar y simplificar las funciones en la educación virtual.

En asociativa y preparación, el docente promueve la comunicación, que incluye el tiempo para ofrecer tutorías, interactuar y evaluar directamente; Esta acción está relacionada con la personalización de la educación, ya que los estudiantes son atendidos de la misma manera en la que buscan vincularse con ellos para que se entiendan e interioricen los métodos y técnicas utilizadas y se obtenga el éxito esperado en el programa proceso de enseñanza y aprendizaje. Esto se logra mediante la interacción entre los usuarios y el docente, basada en el aprendizaje y el trabajo colaborativo para que el proceso de evaluación sea una retroalimentación clara y concreta, que fomente la comparación y la criticidad, permita la negociación y apoye la recuperación. A partir de este último, se generan estrategias de apoyo en las que se abre la motivación.

Por su parte, Álvarez (2008) afirma que una de las principales ventajas de la enseñanza virtual es que facilita la interacción sincrónica y asincrónica, es decir, no está sujeta a restricciones espaciales o temporales. Estas condiciones promueven la autorregulación del aprendizaje, definida por Zimmerman (1990) como aquellos aspectos que contribuyen, de forma cognitivo-metacognitiva, motivacional y conductual, a que el alumno sea un promotor activo de sus propios procesos de aprendizaje. En el aspecto cognitivo-metacognitivo, cuando sean capaces de tomar decisiones que regulen la selección y uso de diferentes formas de conocimiento: planificar, organizar, instruir, controlar y evaluar; en la motivación, cuando son capaces de tener gran autoeficacia, autoatribuciones y gran interés intrínseco en la tarea, destacando el extraordinario esfuerzo y perseverancia durante el aprendizaje; y conductualmente, cuando son capaces de seleccionar, estructurar y crear entornos para optimizar el aprendizaje, buscando consejos, información y lugares donde ver favorecido su aprendizaje; Esto también se logra promoviendo el aprendizaje colaborativo. Las fortalezas de este tipo de aprendizaje se basan en el uso de las estrategias antes mencionadas.

Ahora bien, ¿cómo se logra este proceso en un aula virtual? Una forma de impulsar los procesos de enseñanza y aprendizaje en la virtualidad es la metodología PACIE, que, según Oñate (2009), se utiliza en educación virtual para el uso y aplicación de herramientas virtuales. PACIE significa: P, presencia (institucional en el mundo de Internet); A, alcance (académico, experimental y tutorial); C, formación (motivar y preparar a los docentes en el uso de herramientas tecnológicas que refuercen las cátedras impartidas); Yo, interacción (que permite al docente y alumno llegar a los procesos de comunicación de participación abierta, permanente y colaborativa); E, e-learning (facilita la inclusión de e-learning apoyados en nuevas tecnologías, como Web 2.0, c-learning).

Esta metodología incentiva a los docentes a estructurar su aula tomando en cuenta los siguientes bloques: bloque O, que incluye tres foros virtuales: el primero para la sección de información (información general sobre el curso, objetivos y metas, presentación del tutor y procesos de evaluación); el segundo para el apartado de comunicación (explica el inicio de cada unidad, qué trabajo se hará en la semana, establece fechas para evaluaciones, aclaraciones y pautas para el trabajo de los alumnos); y el tercero presenta un apartado de interacción para generar espacios de apoyo y experiencias positivas; es la base del aprendizaje colaborativo.

El segundo bloque se conoce como académico, el cual contiene la sección expositiva para la presentación de las unidades y contenidos de aprendizaje; la sección de rebote para crear las actividades necesarias para que el alumno lea y asimile los documentos, videos y enlaces web utilizados en la sección expositiva; el apartado de construcción, en el que el alumno debe justificar y defender las posibles soluciones a los temas planteados en el curso; y la sección de verificación, también llamada evaluación; Se presentan actividades que permiten conocer si el alumno aprendió, asimiló y comprendió los contenidos expuestos.

El último bloque es el de cierre y contiene una sección de negociación en la comunidad de aprendizaje, entre tutor y aprendices, directa e indirectamente; Incluye una sección de retroalimentación, en la que el alumno genera información en encuestas para saber si la interacción, la respuesta del tutor y la información fue correcta y significativa. El siguiente gráfico ejemplifica las secciones mencionadas:

Lo anterior destaca que el proceso de enseñanza y aprendizaje virtual involucra y exige un proceso tutorial que considere el diseño de un aula virtual interactiva y atractiva para los estudiantes, con planificación y practicidad de estrategias que se enfoquen en sus necesidades individuales y grupales, con el fin de fomentar la interacción, el placer de aprender y la posibilidad de procesar la información de una forma más significativa y adaptada al contexto social real actual promoviendo el aprendizaje colaborativo.

Aprendizaje colaborativo

Panitz (2008) considera el aprendizaje colaborativo como una filosofía de interacción y una forma de trabajo que implica el desarrollo tanto de conocimientos y habilidades individuales como de una actitud positiva de interdependencia y respeto por las contribuciones del grupo. Es un proceso en el que el conocimiento es descubierto por los estudiantes, reconstruido a través de conceptos que se pueden relacionar y expandir a través de nuevas experiencias de aprendizaje. De ahí que el aprendizaje colaborativo resalte la participación activa del alumno en el proceso de aprendizaje porque el aprendizaje surge de las transacciones entre alumnos y entre profesor y alumnos.

Por su parte, Kaye (2003) afirma que el éxito del aprendizaje colaborativo radica en el objetivo compartido, la interacción, el respeto mutuo y la confianza entre los miembros del grupo de estudiantes, y la creación, manipulación y comunicación en entornos virtuales o no. Así, la base del aprendizaje colaborativo en la educación virtual es la cooperación entre todas las entidades involucradas en el acto didáctico, lo que implica trabajar en conjunto para promover, potenciar y maximizar el aprendizaje significativo de ellas.

Entre las actividades de enseñanza virtual que los docentes pueden utilizar para asesorar y promover este tipo de aprendizajes están: charlas grupales en el aula virtual y en otro medio tecnológico (Messenger, Skype, Twitter, otros), así como la participación en foros virtuales y videoconferencias, entre otros. La acción de todos ellos incentiva a los estudiantes a participar activamente en la discusión de ideas, problemas, propuestas y proyectos que conducen a un consenso grupal para resolver y resolver todas las tareas que se definen en las actividades de aprendizaje; Además, permiten el fortalecimiento de relaciones positivas entre estudiantes, alto rendimiento y desempeño en la realización de actividades que en sí mismas involucran la automotivación y motivación del grupo de estudio.

En este sentido, el rol del docente que promueve este aprendizaje dentro de la educación virtual es el de un mediador que, según Díaz y Hernández (2007), especifica y presenta los objetivos, metas y contenidos al inicio del curso; toma decisiones sobre la formación, el tipo, el tamaño de los grupos y los roles que desempeñarán los estudiantes para asegurar la interdependencia; planifica materiales didácticos con el uso de TIC y estructura el objetivo grupal de interdependencia positiva; explica y monitorea constantemente la tarea educativa y los criterios para el éxito a través de su intervención oportuna y responde preguntas e inquietudes; Evaluar la acción del grupo y valorar el buen funcionamiento del grupo en general.

Las competencias esenciales o f t él Maestro Dentro de Educación Virtual

Para Camacho (2010), el docente debe contar con competencias que le permitan generar una ayuda pedagógica que potencie la permanencia del alumno en el curso virtual evitando el riesgo de deserción, aumentando su satisfacción y aumentando el rendimiento académico;

Además, debe ser hábil en el manejo tecnológico que permita un buen uso de recursos y materiales y superar imprevistos. De esta forma, se pueden caracterizar algunas competencias esenciales para docente de e-learning:

- La necesidad de convertirse en un intermediario entre el estudiante y la institución, para brindar información y asesoría al sistema, ya que la credibilidad en el mismo inicialmente pasará por él.

- Pasar de ser un experto en contenidos a un mediador de aprendizaje, a partir de diseños de experiencia que ofrecen al alumno una estructura inicial para iniciar la interacción.

- Poseer habilidades técnicas mínimas no solo para intervenir en el sistema, sino para resolver las limitaciones que se le presentan al alumno para interactuar en él.

- Presentar los contenidos de los materiales de forma que favorezcan el aprendizaje al máximo cuando su uso es individual y solitario, mediante diseños específicos, una organización lógica de los contenidos e inserciones de bibliografía, resúmenes, mapas conceptuales, definiciones, esquemas, referencias a web. páginas y actividades.

- Potenciar la retroalimentación informativa mediante el envío de mensajes vía campus virtual en base a los comentarios planteados por los alumnos, como reflexiones que surgen de la revisión de trabajos, aclaración de posibles dudas y orientación ante las dificultades.

- Dotar a los estudiantes de recursos suficientes desde materiales en diferentes formatos hasta enlaces a páginas web, para que puedan responder a las demandas y activar los procesos de aprendizaje cognitivo adecuados.

- Proponer un proceso de evaluación del aprendizaje que revele el resultado de la construcción del conocimiento por parte del alumno.

- Establecer una gran cantidad de interacciones con los estudiantes para recopilar información sobre el proceso y la calidad de la construcción del conocimiento que se produce. Estos indicadores deben dar al docente una perspectiva suficientemente amplia sobre el proceso de aprendizaje, de modo que pueda tomar la iniciativa y utilizar metodologías y técnicas de instrucción para apoyar adecuadamente cada proceso de aprendizaje que sigue cada alumno.

- Desplegar un mayor número de ayudas y ver que sean de diferente naturaleza, lo que supone una mayor complejidad en tu actividad docente, ya que muchas veces tendrás que pensar y desarrollar varias formas de presentar un mismo contenido y utilizar estratégicamente varios dispositivos semióticos, según de las necesidades de los estudiantes.

Conclusión

Preguntarse o cuestionarse sobre los principios de una educación pertinente en este tiempo que se vive, preparándose constantemente para el futuro sin vivir ni aprender de la realidad, hace pensar que se vive una inadecuación, en la que el conocimiento se desarticula con la realidad. Cada vez se divide más el conocimiento, mientras que los problemas para abordarlo son transversales; se enseña a abordar un área de conocimiento independientemente de si se puede aplicar en un contexto. En este sentido, el docente de hoy está llamado a utilizar las TIC como un recurso educativo que impulse el desafío de transitar nuevos caminos y experiencias en las que docente y alumnos se hagan corresponsables de alcanzar las metas del conocimiento práctico a través de la autorreflexión y autoevaluación colectiva.

Así, se puede afirmar que la enseñanza y el aprendizaje desde la virtualidad es un medio altamente cualificado para la educación del futuro inmediato, no solo como espacio formativo, sino como proceso de aprendizaje social personalizado y colaborativo, con una acción docente que pretende satisfacer las necesidades e intereses del grupo de estudiantes en la búsqueda del desarrollo de sus habilidades a través de su interacción con el contexto virtual. Todo ello, a través del apoyo mutuo y la colaboración, unido a un clima de libertad, tolerancia y cuidado en el que viven los estudiantes y experimentan que el educador también es educado, que tiene como objetivo generar la autonomía e independencia personal del educando, para que éste pueda transformar su entorno de forma activa y acorde a los avances que presenta la sociedad. Sería, entonces, el reflejo de una enseñanza y aprendizaje virtual proactiva, cooperativa y dinámica que busca la transformación educativa que el contexto social actual necesita. Recuerda que enseñas a aprender y aprendes a enseñar.

Google Classroom: la clase se vuelve digital

Google ofrece herramientas transversales, que pueden utilizarse para las necesidades más habitualescomo organizar tareas diarias, planificar plazos y gestionar su propio material (educativo o no). ¿Te perdiste la primera píldora de capacitación en Google for Education? Aquí está la introducción a Google for Education o siga el curso de Google Suite for Education de ANDI - Asociación Nacional de Profesores de Italiano.

Hoy hablaremos de Google Classroom. Aula compartida en la nube 1 de Google reservada para escuelas. Para acceder a él, solo ingrese sus credenciales y esté habilitado como institución o escuela como se explica en la guía anterior. Las funciones de Google Classroom permiten que las clases se comuniquen, ahorren tiempo y organicen el trabajo. Después de ingresar sus credenciales, puede:

- Inscribirse en un curso, un tablón de anuncios en línea donde se puede compartir comunicaciones personalizadas, textos y pruebas,
- Crear uno desde cero,
- Establecer los permisos (la capacidad de publicar y comentar) de otros usuarios,

- Invitar a una lista de contactos para crear tu propia clase en línea.

Las posibilidades con Google Classroom son numerosas, puedes hacer preguntas a tu clase, reutilizar publicaciones previamente escritas, crear una tarea en línea o crear una comunicación para enviarla directamente a los correos electrónicos de los alumnos. Su uso en la vida cotidiana: con Google Classroom, comunicarte con tus alumnos, configurar tareas y hacerlas visibles incluso para colegas o posibles suplentes es simple. Incluso simplemente compartir un artículo interesante para tus alumnos y leerlo juntos al día siguiente sin tener que imprimir hojas innecesarias que podrían perderse es fácil e intuitivo.

Las escuelas necesitan soluciones simples y fáciles de usar para administrar sus aulas. Con Google Classroom, los profesores pueden asignar asignaciones y tareas a sus alumnos en un instante, lo que fortalece la comunicación y las relaciones entre alumno y profesor. Mejora la implicación directa de los estudiantes, así como la organización y colaboración entre las distintas materias.

Trata de pensar si por un esfuerzo repentino tu plan de enseñanza quedó incompleto y, a tu regreso, los programas de estudio de tus estudiantes se superpusieron con los de los otros maestros. Y ahora trata de imaginar lo fácil que sería organizarte de forma remota (también desde el móvil), asignando tareas y documentación para mantener el aprendizaje constante y comprobar el progreso fácilmente desde casa. O envíe avisos para recordar a los más olvidadizos que debe entregar su permiso de viaje escolar antes del martes y recordar a sus colegas que estará ausente el próximo día para un curso de actualización.

¿Por qué Google Classroom es tan eficiente? Porque compartir las diapositivas, notas y documentos detallados de una lección y ponerlos a disposición también de los alumnos ausentes por motivos de salud se convierte en un juego de niños. Google ha creado un sistema de trabajo centralizado que se convierte en una verdadera herramienta fundamental, indispensable para mantener siempre activa la atención de nuestros alumnos. Cada alumno puede consultar los distintos plazos y gestionar de forma independiente, así como los profesores pueden comprobar en tiempo real quién está haciendo sus deberes, hacer sugerencias y asignar notas:

- Crea contenido multimedia,
- Adjuntar archivos de Google Drive,
- Subir un video,
- Insertar enlaces externos.

T oye ya no son una tarea difícil para los menos experimentados, pero un simple clic desde cualquier dispositivo con conexión a Internet. Para un correcto uso de las aplicaciones de Google para la escuela, que es posible matricularse en el curso en línea en Google suite para la Educación, la cual ofrece un completo de 360 grados de preparación de todas las herramientas que pueda ser utilizado en el aula, incluyendo Google Aula. El curso en línea ilustra todos los pasos y métodos de uso de las funciones múltiples.

AULA DE GOOGLE Y ESCUELA EN CASA

¿Es el aprendizaje en línea tan efectivo como el aprendizaje presencial?

Algunas personas creen que los cursos y exámenes solo pueden tener lugar cuando un "examen real" lleva a los estudiantes dirigidos por un profesor o formador en un lugar determinado, como una clase. Nada más lejos de la realidad. Entonces, comparemos estos dos métodos de aprendizaje.

¿Aprendizaje presencial?

Algunas personas creen que los cursos y exámenes solo pueden tener lugar cuando un "examen real" lleva a los estudiantes dirigidos por un profesor o formador en un lugar determinado, como una clase. Nada más lejos de la realidad. Entonces, comparemos estos dos métodos de aprendizaje.

¿Cuáles son los principales beneficios de la ganancia presencial?

El aprendizaje presencial o "cara a cara" ha sido la normativadurante siglos. Con el aprendizaje presencial los estudiantes interactúan en vivo con el maestro o instructor. Esa interacción ocurre en persona, lo que significa que deben estar físicamente presentes en un aula para aprender. Esto suele suceder en una fecha y hora específicas.

El aprendizaje presencial te ayuda a organizar tus estudios, porque tienes que estar presente en un lugar en un momento específico. Además, puede interactuar con el formador y otros estudiantes. Si no tienes mucha autodisciplina y no haces tu tarea, no hay problema, simplemente siéntate ahí y escucha al profesor hablar.

Además, el aprendizaje presencial se reconoce más ampliamente como un método de aprendizaje "real". Dado que las personas tienen que estar físicamente presentes para los cursos tradicionales, las personas sienten que en realidad se están tomando un tiempo para aprender algo y lo hacen en serio. Empero, enseñar de la manera tradicional no siempre garantiza que la persona esté más enfocada o tenga más éxito.

¿Es el aprendizaje en línea realmente efectivo?

Buena pregunta. A pesar de que estamos en una era moderna en la que no tenemos que estar físicamente presentes en un lugar para aprender algo, las personas todavía luchan por tomar en serio el aprendizaje en línea. Pero echemos un vistazo a los hechos:

- **La mayoría de las personas hoy en día prefiere consumir contenido a través de Internet en** lugar de hacerlo de otra manera. ¡El solo hecho de que estés leyendo esta página es prueba de ello! ¿Por qué el aprendizaje debería seguir siendo estrictamente tradicional mientras todo lo demás parece ir en una dirección diferente?

- **¡El aprendizaje en línea requiere más autodisciplina y sorpresa! incluso puedes aprender más:** como ningún profesor te supervisa, tienes que "supervisarte a ti mismo". Lo que significa que debe tomarse el tiempo para estudiar, prestar atención a lo que está estudiando y aplicar lo que ha aprendido al realizar un examen.

- **Los resultados del examen mostraron que aquellos que estudian de forma remota pueden lograr puntajes similares o mejores que los estudiantes tradicionales en la escuela secundaria y la universidad.** De hecho, muchas de las mejores universidades del mundo ahora ofrecen cursos de educación a distancia.

- **No pierdas tiempo viajando:** con el aprendizaje en línea, no hay necesidad de gastar dinero ni tiempo en transporte. Puedes estudiar usando cualquier medio conectado a Internet.

- **Con el aprendizaje en línea, aún puede obtener un diploma o certificado.** Sí exactamente. Y ese certificado puede ser el mismo que el de los que realizan cursos presenciales.

Entonces, ¿cuál debería elegir?

No digamos que se deba detener el aprendizaje tradicional. Sin embargo, el aprendizaje en línea no solo es una alternativa viable, sino una excelente alternativa. Algunos profesores y formadores prefieren utilizar un enfoque mixto para combinar ambos métodos para maximizar los resultados.

Si eres profesor o formador te recomendamos que consideres los beneficios del aprendizaje online y cómo puede hacerte la vida mucho más fácil sin mermar la calidad.

Google Classroom gratuito para estudiantes y profesores: cómo utilizar la herramienta para estudiar en casa

La plataforma ayuda a organizar actividades y permite descargar archivos, entre otras cosas.

Estudiar en casa es cada vez más fácil con la ayuda de la tecnología, ejemplo de ello son las herramientas de **Google**, las cuales se pusieron a disposición de todos los alumnos, docentes y emprendedores durante esta etapa de encierro creado por coronavirus.

El **gigante tecnológico** compartió una diversidad de cursos a través de internet para alimentar la educación en México.

Tal es el caso **de G Suite** y **Classroom**, que según el secretario de Educación Pública —Esteban Moctezuma— fueron creados para que tanto docentes como alumnos pudieran estudiar de forma gratuita, de tal manera que no hubiera interrupción en su aprendizaje, además en beneficio de los emprendedores.

Google Classroom se creó oficialmente en 2014; sin embargo, se arraigó hasta este **2020 y ganó popularidad entre los estudiantes, ya que no podían asistir a las aulas de las escuelas.**

¿Cómo utilizar la herramienta Classroom?

Toda persona que quiera ocupar Google Classroom deberá identificarse con una cuenta de **Google o Gmail** que deberá crear para poder utilizar dicha plataforma.

Luego debes ingresar a la página de internet **classroom.google.com** donde primero debes verificar la cuenta con la que se identifica el interesado, haciendo clic en continuar.

Luego presiona el botón + ubicado en la parte superior derecha donde puedes **seleccionar la clase** ya creada o crear una nueva. Si escribes uno, se le pedirá la dirección URL de la clase asignada por su profesor.

Al entrar hay varias pestañas que ayudarán al alumno a coordinar y organizar sus tareas y trabajos.

Los archivos también se pueden adjuntar a **través de un enlace, desde la computadora, desde Google Drive o cargar videos de YouTube.**

Con la herramienta puedes crear o seleccionar clases. (Foto: Especial)

Además, se puede ingresar nuevos participantes (estudiantes) y los profesores podrán calificar y cargar trabajos, permitiendo la conexión y supervisión remota de los estudiantes.

¿Qué es G Suite?

G Suite es la otra herramienta de Google que fue diseñada para controlar y administrar empresas con su propio dominio.

En él puedes generar direcciones de correo electrónico profesionales, por ejemplo; yourname @ejemplo.com

En abril, Google compartió una forma más de pasar el tiempo y quedarse en casa durante este período de propagación del COVID-19, y ofreció **clases y cursos para pequeñas** y medianas empresas (PyMEs), para que puedan desarrollar mejores técnicas de aprendizaje y superación.

La iniciativa "**Crece con Google en casa" estaba dirigida a emprendedores, empresarios, empleados, educadores, periodistas, entre otros**, que pudieran acceder a algunas herramientas gratuitas como Google My Business, que sirve para mantener la comunicación con los clientes.

A través de conferencias virtuales en **YouTube**, la plataforma de Internet ofreció **tres sesiones de capacitación.**

"El objetivo de mantenerse conectado, mejorar la productividad en el trabajo y aprender en casa, administrar negocios de forma remota y adquirir nuevas **habilidades digitales**", dijo la compañía en un comunicado.

Los cursos virtuales fueron algunos como: "Herramientas gratuitas de Google para ayudar a tu pyme", en el que se ofreció un curso de tres sesionesde 35 minutos cada unadirigido a pequeños y medianos emprendedores, además de Google for Education para profesores, a través del cual los profesores aprendieron a implementar diversos materiales y estrategias didácticas.

Se recordó la implementación de otras herramientas como: Gmail, Hangouts Meet y Google Drive, Chat, Calendar, Docs. Además de consejos para usarlos de la mejor manera.

Educación virtual: ventajas, mitos y consejos para mejorar los resultados

Puede que ya esté convencido de que la educación virtual es una excelente opción para aprender e impartir conocimientos. O puede ser que aún tengas dudas sobre la efectividad de este tipo de educación y su alcance.

Lo que es un hecho es que la educación virtual sigue ganando popularidad. **Actualmente, más de seis millones de estudiantes toman uno o más cursos en línea**; El 50% de las universidades ofrecen al menos un programa en línea.

... Y estas cifras solo seguirán creciendo a medida que continúe la incorporación de nuevas tecnologías en el mundo actual.

En unos años, este modelo educativo será la regla en todo el mundo.

Dada mi trayectoria como líder en transformación digital universitaria, y en el contexto actual en el que todavía hay personas que no están convencidas de la educación virtual, les comparto este artículo donde enumero los principales beneficios, niego algunos mitos y ofrezco algunos buenos. Prácticas a tener en cuenta.

Principales ventajas de la educación virtual

Si no ha realizado un curso en línea, ¿se ha preguntado alguna vez cómo es realmente la experiencia de aprender virtualmente? Aunque las plataformas de aprendizaje en línea utilizadas pueden diferir ligeramente, la educación virtual ofrece muchos beneficios en comparación con el método de enseñanza tradicional, por ejemplo:

- **Amplia las oportunidades de aprendizaje:** uno de los principales beneficios de la educación virtual es que ofrece una amplia variedad de recursos para el profesor, de las visitas virtuales, bibliotecas en línea con recursos curadas, evaluaciones interactivas, conexiones con expertos de todo el mundo, etc. Con los avances tecnologícos, las clases pueden ser creativas y participativas en todo momento.

- **Aprendes en cualquier lugar:** solo necesita un dispositivo electrónico (teléfono celular, tableta o computadora portátil) para acceder a los materiales de estudio.

- **Puedes elegir cuándo estudiar:** muchos estudiantes trabajan; Por este motivo, **la educación virtual** les permite seguir aprendiendo desde cualquier lugar y en cualquier momento. Un estudio preguntó a los estudiantes por qué eligen aprender en línea. La mayoría respondió que debido a la conveniencia y flexibilidad que ofrecen los programas. Un 59%, es decir, mas de la mitad de los estudiantes encuestados tienen hijos y lamitad de todos los estudiantes informó que también tienen un trabajo.

- **Responsabilidad y autonomía:** crear una rutina y realizar las actividades correspondientes es un buen consejo para completar con éxito los programas ofertados.

Rompiendo mitos para aumentar el alcance educativo

A pesar del crecimiento exponencial de la educación virtual, muchas personas todavía la consideran un tipo de educación inferior.

Estoy aquí para decirles que estas creencias están lejos de la verdad y que la educación en línea puede ser tan creíble, confiable, beneficiosa y efectiva como la educación tradicional.

Por eso, me gustaría aprovechar esta oportunidad para desacreditar los 3 mitos más comunes.

Mito 1. La calidad de la educación virtual es inferior

Esto es falso, porque la educación virtual se compone de muchos factores de calidad. Por ejemplo:

- El tutor es un especialista en las áreas en las que imparte docencia.

- Las herramientas tecnológicas están especializadas para brindar un excelente servicio.
- Las clases se planifican a través de programas educativos probados y efectivos.
- La atención que se brinda a los alumnos es personalizada.

Mito 2. Los maestros no están capacitados para enseñar en línea

Muchas veces escuchas este tipo de expresiones sin fundamento. Sin embargo, considero que las demandas y desafíos de la nueva sociedad del conocimiento exigen competencias diferentes a los docentes. El rol tradicional del docente cambia en la modalidad virtual, para convertirse en un tutor que facilita y acompaña al alumno en su proceso de construcción de conocimientos, respetando su autonomía.

> *El rol tradicional del docente cambia en la modalidad virtual, para convertirse en un tutor que facilita y acompaña al alumno en su proceso de construcción de conocimientos, respetando su autonomía.*

Mito 3. La educación virtual es una moda

Mucha gente cree que esta es una tendencia global que pronto pasará. Sin embargo, es falso que la educación virtual sea una moda que desaparecerá con los años.

Un factor clave para que las universidades ofrezcan clases en línea es mantenerse al día con las nuevas expectativas de los estudiantes. En esencia, aquellas universidades que no ofrecen educación virtual enfrentan una desventaja competitiva dentro de una población estudiantil que necesita y espera poder aprender en línea, desde cualquier lugar.

Las nuevas generaciones optan cada vez más por este modelo de aprendizaje. Algunas de las razones son:

- El acceso a la educación existe para todas las personas, especialmente para quienes trabajan.
- El uso de las TIC permite incrementar el aprendizaje y la comunicación de los estudiantes, ya que con el uso de dispositivos móviles, plataformas digitales y/o aplicaciones, la información se comparte de forma inmediata y se puede acceder a ella desde cualquier lugar.
- Con el uso de plataformas educativas virtuales, el aula física se convierte en una opción. Muchos de los estudiantes que tienen diversas actividades en su vida diaria pueden acceder a una sala virtual donde se les brinda una atención personalizada, lo que les permite desarrollar sus habilidades y conocimientos con mayor rendimiento.

Consejos para afrontar con éxito el reto de la educación virtual

Así como la educación virtual tiene muchos beneficios, también enfrentamos algunos desafíos. Algunas universidades están utilizando métodos innovadores para fomentar una experiencia educativa en línea que sea más inclusiva, atractiva y receptiva a las demandas de los estudiantes.

Ten en cuenta los siguientes consejos:

1. **El contenido creado por los profesores debe estar diseñado específicamente para el entorno virtual.** Teniendo en cuenta que las aulas virtuales o los cursos de aprendizaje en línea difieren de los cursos presenciales, el contenido también debe ser diferente. Se recomienda que sea más breve e interactivo. Por ejemplo, es importante ofrecer materiales de referencia adicionales en determinadas secciones o incluso enlaces externos. Esto hace que el contenido se adapte a las diferentes necesidades de los estudiantes.

2. **Concéntrate en el aprendizaje activo.** Incluso los profesores más divertidos y entretenidos no pueden permitirse crear lecciones pasivas en línea. El curso debe ser interactivo. Se debe incluir un buen número de oportunidades para la participación de los estudiantes, por ejemplo, combinando discusiones, colaboración, clips de video y audio, y ejercicios prácticos con texto y posiblemente conferencias

breves en video. Ningún alumno permanecerá atento e interesado durante mucho tiempo sin interactividad.

3. **La "presencia docente" juega un papel vital en la construcción de un sentido de pertenencia** a la comunidad de aprendizaje y en mantener a los estudiantes interactuando activamente con el contenido. Muchas investigaciones han revelado que recibir comentarios y comunicaciones constantes del maestro puede marcar una gran diferencia en la confianza, la motivación y el desempeño de estos estudiantes en el curso.

4. **Los estudiantes tienen diferentes estilos de aprendizaje.** En este sentido, es pertinente identificar cómo tus alumnosaprenden mejor y así utilizar diferentes herramientas para adaptarse a diferentes estilos. Recomiendo usar una combinación de varios medios, incluidos texto, video, audio, infografías, presentaciones, gamificación y más; se ha descubierto que esto es más efectivo que incluir solo texto y audio.

5. **Lecciones por segmentos.** Las clases largas de 2 a 3 horas sin descansos probablemente no son la mejor manera de impartir un curso presencial, y hacerlo en línea es aún más ineficiente.Recomiendo presentar la información de 10 minutos s segmentos y como he mencionado antes, en la variación del formato.

Con esta información es posible mejorar el alcance y los resultados de **la educación virtual** en todos los niveles.

CAPÍTULO 3:
VISIÓN DEL PROFESOR

AULA DE GOOGLE PARA PROFESORES

El **coronavirus** está provocando que se dispare el número de estudiantes que enseñan desde casa. Existen muchas alternativas para la **enseñanza a distancia online** pero una de las más populares en los últimos días es **Google Classroom**. Te explicamos cómo utilizarlo y todos sus detalles.

Google Classroom se lanzó en agosto de 2014 y desde 2017 puede ser utilizado por cuentas personales de Google sin tener que tener una suscripción a G Suite. Inicialmente, fue diseñado con el objetivo de ahorrar papel, pero su utilidad ha superado su uso inicial para distribuir tareas o evaluar contenidos. Como su nombre lo indica, permite contar con aulas virtuales, permitiendo no solo a profesores y alumnos una interacción más fluida a distancia, sino que los padres puedan estar más informados de todo el proceso educativo. Y como vamos a ver, probablemente sea la mejor herramienta que tenemos para enseñar online, ya que también nos permite unirnos a Hangouts Meet para realizar videollamadas y tener una experiencia de **aula virtual** completa.

Crear y configurar clases

Acceder a Google Classroom es realmente sencillo. Solo tenemos que crear acceso a **classroom.google.com** con nuestro correo electrónico, ya sea nuestra cuenta personal o una que hayamos creado específicamente para clases si no queremos revelar la nuestra. A partir de ahí, estaremos dentro.

En la parte superior derecha tenemos un icono de "+" en el que podemos unirnos a una clase si somos alumnos, o crear una clase si somos profesores. En el caso de que seamos docentes, es importante que sepamos que si vamos a enseñar en un centro educativo con alumnos, tendremos que tener una cuenta creada para G Suite for Education al Centres, que es gratuita.

Para crear una clase, podemos crear una clase, una sección, una asignatura y un nombre de clase. Gracias a esto, los estudiantes pueden identificar fácilmente materias y clases. A partir de ahí, ya tendremos nuestra clase creada, con el Código de Clase que tendremos que entregar a los alumnos para que puedan entrar en ella.

En este panel podemos seleccionar la asignatura de la clase, subir una foto personalizada, enviar mensajes a todos los alumnos, crear trabajos de clase con tareas y preguntas y organizar el trabajo.También podemos gestionar alumnos y profesores con acceso de **personas**, y finalmente también podemos juzgar el trabajo de los alumnos en el apartado **Valoración**.

En el panel podemos seleccionar la asignatura de la clase, subir una foto personalizada, enviar mensajes a todos los alumnos, crear trabajos de clasecon tareas y preguntas y organizar el trabajo.También podemos gestionar alumnos y profesores con acceso de **personas**, y finalmente también podemos juzgar el trabajo de los alumnos en la sección **Valoraciones**.

En la sección para crear puestos de trabajo, podemos elegir las tareas, cuestionarios, preguntas, materiales, etc. Podemos asignar puntos a cada tarea, y las fechas de entrega establecida. En el caso de las tareas con cuestionarios, se pueden realizar mediante cuestionarios de Google.

Invitar a tus alumnos a Google Classroom

Hola, bienvenido a otro tutorial paso a paso en Google Classroom. La última vez, aprendimos cómo crear un Google Classroom hoy I.

En este tutorial, veremos cómo invitar a los estudiantes a unirse a su Google Classroom. Hay dos formas de invitar a los alumnos a tu Google Classroom: mostrando el código de la clase o invitándolos directamente.

Para invitar a estudiantes por código de clase, inicia sesión en tu Google Classroom. Selecciona un aula a la que te gustaría invitar a tus alumnos. El código de tu clase se muestra justo debajo de su nombre, haz clic en Mostrar y asegúrate de que el código de la clase sea visible para tus alumnos. Puedes proyectarlo en la pantalla o simplemente escribirlo en la pizarra.

Cambiemos a la vista de un alumno para ver lo que deberán hacer desde allí y poder usar este código de clase para unirse a tu Google Classroom.

Indica a tus alumnos que inicien sesión en Google utilizando sus cuentas de Gmail de la escuela. También indicales que vayan al aula virtual, hagan clic en el botón derechoen la esquina superior, y este es el momento en el que insertarán un código de clase. Una vez que hayan terminado, deben hacer clic en unirse. Eso es todo, un estudiante se ha unido con éxito a su Google Classroom.

Ahora volvamos a la vista del profesor para ver qué ha cambiado en nuestro Google Classroom. Si vas a la pestaña de personas, deberían poder ver a los estudiantes que se han unido con éxito a tu aula. El código de clase es una forma fácil y directa de invitar a tus alumnos a unirse a un código de clase de Google Classroom que no cambia con el tiempo. Es permanente y está asignado a Google Classroom. Puedes usarlo en otro momento si hay estudiantes que estuvieron ausentes mientras mostraba el código de la clase.

La invitación directa es otra forma de llenar tu Google Classroom. Para hacer eso, abre tu aula de Google, selecciona una clase a la que te gustaría invitar a tus estudiantes a ir a la pestaña "personas". Busca el letrero para invitar a los estudiantes y haz clic en él. Este es el campo donde pegarás o ingresarás nombres o correos electrónicos de los estudiantes a quienes le gustaría invitar. Una vez que hayas terminado, haz clic en invitar. Una vez que se haya enviado la invitación, verás el nombre de los estudiantes en gris. Esto indica que han recibido la invitación pero aún no se han unido a una clase.

Cambiemos a una vista de estudiante para ver qué deben hacer desde allí y poder aceptar la invitación y unirse a tu salón de clases. Indica a tus alumnos que inicien sesión en Google utilizando sus cuentas escolares. Una vez que hayan iniciado sesión, indícales que vayan a Google Classroom. Una vez allí, deberían poder ver un Google Classroom, al que los invitó. En mi caso, es mi primer Google Classroom. El último paso que deben tomar es hacer clic en unirse, y eso es todo.Tu alumno se ha unido con éxito a tu Google Classroom por invitación directa.

Regresemos a la vista de los profesores para ver qué ha cambiado y el nombre que solía estar atenuado ahora es negro sólido. Si el nombre aún aparece en gris claro, significa que un estudiante aún no ha aceptado tu invitación.

Bueno, felicidades, ahora sabes cómo invitar a los estudiantes a unirse a tu Google Classroom mediante el código de clase o invitándolos directamente. En nuestro próximo paso, tutoriales paso a paso de Google Classroom, veremos cómo crear y recopilar tareas de los estudiantes.

Cómo crear y recopilar tareas de los estudiantes

Hoy veremos cómo crear y recopilar asignaciones. Sin más preámbulos, entremos en ello.

Para crear una tarea, ve al trabajo de clase y haz clic en "Crear tarea". Asigna un título a la tarea, escribe las instrucciones para tus alumnos. Selecciona si deseas que tu tarea será calificada o clasificadas. Selecciona una fecha límite para tu tarea. Hablaremos deeste tema en otro tutorial. Así que por ahora, no dejes temas.

Hay cuatro tipos de materiales complementarios que puedes adjuntar a tu tarea. El primero es un archivo adjunto desde tu ordenador o un archivo, el segundo es un archivo de Google Drive. El tercero es un videoclip de YouTube. El cuarto está vinculado a cualquier recurso que se encuentre en Internet. Para mi tarea, decidí usar los cuatro.

Para adjuntar archivos desde mi computadora, haré clic en el primer icono. Selecciona archivos de mi dispositivo, selecciono un archivo, hago clic en Abrir. Luego hago clic en Cargar. Ahora mi tarea tiene una imagen que adjunté desde mi computadora.

Para un videoclip de YouTube, encontré un clip sobre "creatividad" que me gustaría que mis alumnos vieran. Selecciono el clip que me gustaría que los estudiantes vieran y haz clic en 'Agregar'. Ahora la tarea tiene un videoclip de YouTube. Pero también tengo una charla TED que me gustaría que mis alumnos vieran. Así que haré clic en el cuarto icono (unidad de Google) y pegaré mi enlace aquí. Haz clic en Agregar vínculo.

Finalmente, me gustaría que mis alumnos pudieran reflexionar sobre todos los materiales que han visto. A estos efectos, yo creé un documento de Google Docs. Así que haré clic en el segundo icono y seleccionaré un documento de Google que he creado recientemente para esta tarea. Selecciona el archivo de tu Google Drive y haz clic en Agregar. Una cosa importante que debe recordar al asignar Google Docs a sus clases es seleccionar el tipo de uso compartido apropiado.

Hay tres tipos, los estudiantes pueden ver el archivo, los estudiantes pueden editar el archivo y hacer una copia para cada estudiante. Permítanme describir brevemente cada uno de ellos. Si seleccionas estudiantes que pueden ver el archivo, los estudiantes solo podrán ver el documento de Google que ha conectado. Entonces, en mi caso, no es una opción porque quiero que realmente escriban una mejor reflexión. Los estudiantes pueden editar el archivo significa que todos los estudiantes editarán un archivo en lo que se adapte a mis propósitos, ya sea porque quiero que cada estudiante individual escribe tu propio reflejo. La tercera opción parece tener más sentido "hacer una copia para cada alumno". Google Classroom duplicará esta tarea y hará una copia separada de.

Cada estudiante que parece justo antes de hacer clic en Asignar, todavía hay una característica más de la que aún no hemos hablado de varias asignaciones. Si estás enseñando más de una clase, puedes beneficiarte de esta función. La asignación múltiple es básicamente significa que asigna la misma asignación a múltiples clases. Para hacer eso, despláza hacia arriba y hazclic en y simplemente selecciona las clases a las que te gustaría asignar esta tarea. Por lo tanto, también puedes seleccionar a todos los estudiantes o puedes tomar estudiantes individuales. Una vez que hayas hecho todo lo posible, puedes asignar la tarea de inmediato, programar la asignación para que se asigne más tarde, guardarla como borrador y finalizarla más tarde. En mi caso, asignaré esta tarea de inmediato.

Felicidades, acaba de crear tu primera asignación, i recauciones, recursos, y el recuento de los estudiantes. Es importante comprender qué significa "entregar" y asignar significa "tarea" significa cuántos estudiantes se les ha asignado esta tarea mientras solo hay dos estudiantes en mi clase. Entonces, el número dos está aquí, se determina cuántos estudiantes han completado y devuelto sus tareas. Y así es como se ve la tarea desde su final. Pero, ¿por qué no cambiamos de perspectiva y vemos qué aspecto tienen los estudiantes?

Y ahora para hacer eso, vamos a imaginar que ahora soy un estudiante. Y voy a iniciar sesión en el aula, en mi registro Google aula y ver lo que parece. Ahora, para hacer eso, voy a abrir Google, tienen una entrada en mi Google Classroom y selecciono mi Google Classroom. Cuando los estudiantes abren tu Google Classroom, inmediatamente inician sesión en la transmisión, que es básicamente un suministro de noticias de lo que está sucediendo y lo nuevo. Puedo ver aquí que un maestro publicó una nueva tarea, también puedo ver las próximas fechas de entrega. Entonces, para abrir las asignaciones, puedo hacer clic en la tarea en mi flujo o puedo ir a' trabajo de clase' y seleccionar mi tarea. Desde aquí, puedo ver el nombre de la tarea, las instrucciones y todos los recursos. Bueno, mi tarea es escribir una reflexión sobre la importancia de la creatividad del siguiente tema.' Imaginemos que tengo acceso a todos estos recursos. Y ahora estoy listo para escribir por reflexión. Bueno, para ello abro el Google Doc que me ha asignado un profesor anteriormente. Puedes ver en la pantalla que Google Classroom he creado un documento separado para mí y asígnarle el nombre correspondiente. Una vez que un alumno está listo, es importante devolver la tarea en el botón "entregar" que se encuentra en la esquina superior derecha. Voy a hacer clic en entregar. Google Classroom me preguntará, ¿voy a entregar este trabajo? Sí, voy a entregar este trabajo. Eso es. Mi tarea ha sido enviada.

Ahora volvamos al lado del profesor para ver qué ha cambiado. Puedes ver en mi pantalla que un estudiante se ha transmitido a entregado. Ahora tengo un estudiante al que se le asignó la tarea pero aún no la ha completado. También tengo otro estudiante que completó esta tarea y la entregó porque esta tarea está calificada. Mi trabajo como profesor ahora es dar una calificación a esta tarea y devolvérsela al alumno. Para hacerlo, haz clic en "entregado".

Este es el nombre del estudiante que ha completado tu tarea, haz clic en la tarea. Como profesor, tienes muchas características cuando se trata de calificar. Puedes dejar un comentario, puedes sugerir nuevas ideas, pero este es un tema para otro tutorial. Ahora mismo vamos a ver esta tarea. Démosle a este estudiante 80 sobre 100.

Una vez que hayas hecho eso, haz clic en regresar. Confirma tu devolución. Eso es todo. Tu trabajo como profesor está hecho. Has asignado el trabajo que has marcado y devuelto el trabajo. Ahora regresemos a la vista de los estudiantes para ver qué ha cambiado. Como estudiante, ahora puedo ver mi calificación 80 de 100. Hay muchas otras características útiles cuando se trata de calificar el trabajo de los estudiantes, pero las veremos en otra sección.

De modo que ha aprendido a asignar, recopilar y devolver el trabajo de los estudiantes. En nuestra siguiente sección, veremos cómo asignar tareas de prueba a través de Google Classroom.

Cómo utilizar la "preguntas"

¿Es eres uno de esos educadores que les gustaría involucrar a sus estudiantes en discusiones en línea significativas y productivas, pero simplemente no sabe por dónde empezar, qué plataforma usar y qué sitio web ir? Y simplemente vuelve a escribir con lápiz todo el tiempo para este tipo de tareas. Bueno, buenas noticias. Al final de esta sección, podrás involucrar a tus estudiantes en discusiones en línea significativas, fluidas y auténticas con la ayuda del panel de discusión de Google en el aula.

Si no está familiarizado con Google Classroom, consulte las secciones anteriores de este libro sobre cómo comenzar. Si ya tiene un Google Classroom, profundicemos.

Lo primero que debe hacer es ir al trabajo de clase desde la pantalla de inicio de Google Classroom. Desde allí, seleccione Crear, seleccione pregunta. Así es como iniciamos un foro de discusión.

Lo primero en lo que debemos pensar es en qué queremos que hablen nuestros estudiantes. Y esta va a ser nuestra pregunta. Bueno, en mi caso, quiero que mis alumnos discutan un videoclip que encontré en YouTube sobre "creatividad". Quiero que compartan sus ideas. Entonces esta será mi pregunta "comparta sus ideas sobre el video adjunto", haré clic en el signo de YouTube y adjuntaré el videoclip que me gustaría que mis alumnos discutan, compartan, percepciones, seleccione el clip, haz clic Añadir. Entonces tengo mi pregunta. Aquí tengo mi clip. Y la otra cosa que debemos seleccionar es cómo responderán los estudiantes a esta pregunta. Tenemos dos opciones. Podemos aceptar respuestas cortas o de opción múltiple. Bueno, en nuestro caso, queremos iniciar un foro de discusión. Así que la respuesta corta tiene más sentido.

Asegúrte de permitir que los alumnos se respondan entre sí. Esto permitirá que los estudiantes se vean y se respondan los unos a los otros. Los estudiantes pueden editar la respuesta. Normalmente la dejo activada, esta opción permite a los estudiantes volver atrás y editar las respuestas después de que se hayan publicado en caso de que hayan cometido un error tipográfico, hayan cometido un error, puedan volver atrás y editar. Selecciona las clases a las que deseas asignar esta pregunta. Si no lo sabías, puedes asignar simultáneamente la misma tarea a diferentes clases. En mi caso, esto se asignará solo a mi única clase. Y también puedes seleccionar alumnos en mi caso, tengo dos alumnos.

Así que voy a seleccionar a todos los estudiantes, mi tarea no se calificará, no habrá una fecha límite y no habrá ningún tema. Así que dicho eso, todos estamos bien. Podemos preguntar ahora, en este caso, la tarea la publicará de inmediato. Podemos programar esta tarea para un uso posterior, o podemos guardarla como borrador y tal vez pedirla más tarde o editarla más tarde. En mi caso, te lo voy a preguntar ahora.

Una vez que hayas hecho tu pregunta, aparecerá en tu trabajo de clase o en tus novedades. Así es como se ve la tarea. La pregunta estará justo aquí tenemos el videoclip. Y hasta ahora, no tengo a nadie respondido. Tengo dos preguntas. Tengo dos estudiantes a los que se les ha pedido esta tarea, pero no tengo estudiantes que la hayan entregado. Entonces, ¿por qué no vemos cómo se ve esta pregunta de los estudiantes?

Entonces, como estudiante, esto es lo que parece desde mi punto de vista. En mis novedades, puedo ver una pregunta que ha publicado unprofesor. También puedo ir al trabajo de clase y ver esta pregunta allí. Intentemos tocarlo.

Así es como se ve la pregunta, tengo la pregunta justo en la parte superior y puedo hacer tres cosas. Puedo agregar un comentario de clase, puedo escribir mi respuesta o puedo agregar un comentario privado. Y estas tres cosas son ligeramente diferentes entre sí. Entonces, ¿por qué no empezamos escribiendo la respuesta primero una respuesta a la pregunta? Entonces, la pregunta era compartir mis ideas sobre el video adjunto. Entonces mi idea sería que este video es genial. Voy a hacer clic en entregar. Y notarán que una vez que me entregue, ahora puedo ver las respuestas de los compañeros de clase. Si hago clic en ver las respuestas de los compañeros de clase, hasta ahora solo puedo ver mi respuesta. También puedo ver cuántas respuestas tengo aquí mismo. Hasta ahora no tengo respuestas. Ahora intentemos agregar un comentario de clase que se verá diferente a la respuesta a la pregunta. Entonces, mi comentario de clase será, "esta es una tarea increíble", haciendo clic allí mismo. Además de eso, puedo agregar un comentario privado, un comentario privado en lugar de un comentario de clase, y mi respuesta solo la verá mi maestro. Si agrego un comentario privado, puedo decir "este es mi comentario privado para un maestro", haz clic en este botón aquí. Estoy usando la aplicación Google Classroom en este iPad, que se ve un poco diferente a cuando usas Google Classroom en el navegador de Internet.

Muy bien, lo que hemos hecho hasta ahora, hemos agregado nuestra respuesta. Agregamos un comentario de clase y agregamos un comentario privado. Veamos ahora cómo se ve desde la cuenta de otro estudiante. Las mismas opciones disponibles para mí. Puedo agregar un comentario de clase. Puedo decir mi respuesta. Puedo agregar un comentario privado. Y pueden notar que ya tengo un comentario de clase que fue hecho por otro estudiante. "Esta es una tarea increíble". No veo su comentario privado que fue dirigido a un maestro. Entonces, primero escribiré mi respuesta para poder ver las respuestas de todos los estudiantes. "Creo queeste video está desactualizado". Esta es mi opinión.

Entonces, una vez que hayas hecho eso, haz clic en girar. Observa que ahora puedo ver las respuestas de mis compañeros de clase si toco las respuestas de mis compañeros de clase, ahora puedo ver mi respuesta, que es MSCI dos. Creo que este video está desactualizado, pero también puedo ver una respuesta de otro estudiante, Ms one iPad one "Este video es genial". Y lo que puedo hacer, podría hacer clic en el signo de respuesta e iniciar una discusión. Mi respuesta sería "Me gusta tu idea", publícala. Puedes volver al primer alumno, ahora puedo tener una respuesta y puedo hacer clic en esta respuesta y ver la respuesta de otro alumno. Así es como puedes iniciar debates. Si voy a la cuenta de mi tutor, ahora puedo ver que tengo dos estudiantes que entregaron la tarea. Puedo ver un comentario de la clase aquí. Si toco en ver respuestas. Puedo ver los comentarios privados justo debajo del nombre del estudiante al tocar el estudiante uno, un estudiante que tiene un comentario privado. Este es mi comentario privado para el profesor, puedo responder en privado. "Gracias por tu comentario privado". Este comentario irá directamente a este alumno. Así es como se verá la comunicación entre un estudiante y tu, y también entre los estudiantes cuando inicie el panel de discusión de Google en el aula.

Todavía hay una cosa que puede hacer para tener un poco más de control sobre los estudiantes. Si vas a las respuestas de los estudiantes y haces clic en tres puntos. Puedes silenciar a esos estudiantes. Los estudiantes silenciados aún pueden enviar trabajos, pero otros estudiantes no lo verán, no pueden responder a sus compañeros de clase, pueden comentar las publicaciones. Ves lo que está pasando aquí. Si algunos de los estudiantes comienzan a hacer publicaciones tontas y comentarios tontos, puedes silenciarlos y estarán trabajando solos. No podrán ver el trabajo de nadie. No podrán interferir, estarán trabajando solos, pero aún así podrás recoger tu tarea. Así que este es un tipo de moderación que puedes integrar con el foro de discusión en el aula de Google.

Ahora bien, la última cosa que quiero dejar es a veces confunden los estudiantes de clase comentario s y respuesta a la pregunta. Lo que hago personalmente es que deshabilito los comentarios de la clase, porque cuando inicias un panel de discusión, es un poco confuso para los estudiantes si deben publicar un comentario de la clase o si deben responder la pregunta.

Por ello, normalmente desactivo esos comentarios de la clase y el panel de discusión funciona mucho mejor. Bueno, para deshabilitar los comentarios de la clase, vaya a la pantalla de inicio de Google Classroom, haz clic en el botón de engranaje, desplácese un poco hacia abajo hasta las novedades, los estudiantes pueden publicar y comentar y seleccionar "solo los profesores pueden publicar y comentar" y haz clic en Guardar.

Como maestro, yo todavía soy capaz de enviar comentarios clase, pero los alumnos sólo puedo responder a la pregunta, ya sea o añadir un comentario privado o responder a mensajes de otros estudiantes. Ahora ya conoces todos los pasos para comenzar a debatir sobre tableros en Google Classroom.

En nuestra próxima clase de Google, tutoriales en video paso a paso, veremos la mejor manera de compartir materiales y recursos con sus estudiantes.

Cómo utilizar las rúbricas

Hoy, veremos la nueva característica de las rúbricas de Google Classroom. Google ha anunciado esta función recientemente y, en el momento de la grabación, todavía está en desarrollo, se ha dado acceso a algunos probadores y he tenido la suerte de ser uno de ellos. Así que estoy muy emocionado de compartir con ustedes lo que Google ha preparado para nosotros. Si está leyendo esta sección cuando se lanzó esta función, entonces eres afortunado y puedes seguirme. Si estás leyendo esta sección cuando esta función no se ha lanzado, bueno, mírela como una ventaja para prepararse cuando esté disponible.

Entonces, sin más preámbulos, echemos un vistazo a la nueva función de Google Classroom: las rúbricas.

Si vamos a la tarea, verá un nuevo letrero que se ha agregado a la interfaz de usuario a la derecha del tema. Lo primero que debe hacer es crear un título porque no tengo rúbricas, voy a crear una rúbrica desde cero.

Usaré esta rúbrica para calificar el ensayo del estudiante. Entonces, mi primer criterio será la elección de palabras. Voy a asignar tres puntos para el nivel tres. Y esto va a ser una descripción, un uso preciso del vocabulario. Por el bien del tiempo, voy a mantener mi descripción muy simple. Mi segundo nivel costará dos puntos, será el nivel dos, y la descripción será el uso promedio del vocabulario. Mi tercer nivel le dará al estudiante un punto, será el nivel uno y la descripción será un mal uso del vocabulario. Para agregar un nivel hacemos clic en el botón más para el nivel de líder, necesitamos hacer clic en tres puntos y eliminar el nivel.

Mi primer criterio está listo, puedo agregar un nuevo criterio y si hago clic en él, se generará un nuevo campo para otro criterio o lo que puedo hacer puedo duplicar este criterio y simplemente cambiar la elección de palabras. Lo cambiaré a gramática y modificaré un poco mi descripción. La primera descripción será un uso preciso de la gramática.

La segunda descripción va a ser normal, puedo duplicar la gramática y elegir "Opinión". El primer nivel va a funcionar por un punto, luego tres, dos y uno. Las rúbricas de Google generan automáticamente la puntuación máxima. Tengo tres puntos en elección de palabras, tres puntos en gramática y cuatro puntos en opinión, lo que me da 10 puntos. Una vez que mi rúbrica esté lista, haré clic en Guardar.

Una vez que guardes la rúbrica, se podrá ver en la tarea, se puede hacer clic en la rúbrica, así es como se verá. Tienes la opción de borrar los criterios, expandirlos uno por uno o expandirlos todos a la vez. Una vez que la tarea esté lista, haz clic en 'asignar'. Se ha generado la asignación. ¿Por qué no echamos un vistazo a esta tarea y la rúbrica del final de los estudiantes?

Entonces, como estudiante, puedo ver que un maestro ha publicado una nueva tarea. Puedo ver mi flujo de trabajo o puedo ir a mi trabajo de clase y ver sus tareas para la prueba de hobby primero.

Fíjate que cuando abrí esta tarea es que tiene una rúbrica. Si hago clic alrededor de la rúbrica, no hay nada que pueda hacer realmente. Pero esta, la rúbrica es una buena manera de que sus estudiantes sepan lo que se espera de ellos. Sé lo que tengo que hacer para obtener 10 mi. Necesito asegurarme de que mi vocabulario es correcto, mi gramática es precisa y no tengo una descripción para opinar, pero deberían estar ahí. Entonces, ¿por qué no intentamos enviar nuestro trabajo para que un maestro pueda calificar? Vamos a imaginar que la tarea de la rúbrica es mi ensayo.

Ahora mi tarea está entregada y es hora de que un profesor comercialice. Entonces, desde la pantalla del maestro, haz clic en 'entregado' y vea la presentación del estudiante. Este es el estudiante que envió su trabajo como junior. Ahora puedo usar la rúbrica que creé para esta tarea para marcar el trabajo de los estudiantes para ver simultáneamente el trabajo de los estudiantes y marcarlo con la rúbrica. Necesito hacer clic en la herramienta de calificación. Mi rúbrica aparecerá a la derecha, justo en el lado derecho de la pantalla. Puedo expandir cada nivel y comercializar en consecuencia. Entonces, lo que hemos hecho en este momento, hemos analizado el trabajo de los estudiantes y lo hemos marcado al mismo tiempo usando nuestra rúbrica, notará que la rúbrica de Google ha generado una puntuación total de siete sobre 10. Según los niveles que hemos seleccionado. Lo que no hizo, sin embargo, no transfirió la puntuación de la rúbrica a la calificación. La rúbrica de Google transfiere automáticamente la puntuación de la rúbrica a la calificación final.

Entonces, una vez que lo hayamos hecho, como de costumbre, haremos clic en regresar y el trabajo se devolverá al estudiante. Así que volvamos a la vista de los estudiantes para ver qué ha cambiado desde su perspectiva. Puedo hacer clic en la rúbrica y ver de dónde proviene mi puntuación. Mi elección de palabras obtuvo dos puntos, mi gramática me ganó dos puntos, en mi opinión, son mis tres puntos para un total de siete. No puedo ver una puntuación final de la rúbrica, debería ser siete sobre 10 aquí. Y también puedo ver mi puntuación final de 70 sobre 100.

Estoy muy emocionado de compartir esta función contigo. Y creo que esto tiene un gran potencial para agilizar el flujo de trabajo de un estudiante, aumentar la transparencia en términos de expectativas y de dónde proviene la puntuación. Es una adición realmente agradable a Google Classroom.

CAPÍTULO 4:
VISTA DEL ESTUDIANTE

Google Classroom para estudiantes: acceso a Google Classroom

En esta página encontrarás las instrucciones para realizar las **primeras operaciones en Google Classroom:** acceder, ver tareas y materiales, devolver las tareas al profesor. Classroom te permite realizar muchas otras operaciones: consulta en primer lugar a tus profesores, quienes te mostrarán el método de trabajo adecuado para tu clase. También puedes encontrar muchos tutoriales en línea que explican todas las funciones de Classroom de una manera sencilla; algunos también se indican al final de esta página.

Como siempre, acceder desde una computadora o teléfono inteligente/tableta es ligeramente diferente. Aquí tienes diferentes indicaciones según el dispositivo que uses. Si usas tabletas o teléfonos inteligentes, primero lea la sección Desde la computadora, que explica todos los pasos y formas de realizar las diversas operaciones en Classroom; luego mire la sección Desde el móvil, donde encontrará solo las diferencias en comparación con las pantallas de las computadoras.

DE COMPUTADORA

Iniciar sesión en Classroom

- Usa el navegador Chrome
- Ve a google.it
- Asegúrate de haber iniciado sesión con tu cuenta de G Suite o inicie sesión
- Haz clic en la parte superior derecha en el icono con los 9 puntos y elige Classroom
- Si no encuentras el icono, puede escribir directamente en la barra de direcciones de classroom.google.com
- Cuando entres a Classroom verás todos los cursos a los que te han añadido tus profesores: están organizados como grandes cuadrados independientes
- Para participar en un curso debes aceptar la invitación del profesor. Cuando vea un curso con el botón azul Suscribirse, haz clic; si no ves ese botón, significa que ya estás registrado:

Para ingresar al curso, simplemente haz clic en el título del curso, dentro del cuadro de la derecha. En la pantalla que se abre puedes encontrar tareas y materiales de dos formas diferentes. Si mira hacia arriba, verá las dos pestañas del curso Stream y Jobs:

En la pestaña Flujo, la que aparece primero cuando ingresa al curso, encontrará la tarea, los materiales y los comentarios del maestro en orden cronológico inverso.

Como en las redes sociales, encontrarás las últimas novedades en la parte superior, ya medida que vayas bajando encontrarás las anteriores. Entonces, si deseas ver nuevas asignaciones o materiales, esta tarjeta es la más adecuada.

A la derecha, tiene un cuadro que te recuerda si tiene tareas que están por completar.

En la pestaña Trabajos del curso encontrarás los mismos materiales y tareas (no los comentarios y anuncios en su lugar), pero en un orden diferente: están ordenados en la forma en que el profesor decidió y se pueden agrupar por temas.

Si deseas buscar material o asignación por tema, esta pestaña puede ser más útil porque está mejor organizada.

Mira los materiales

Las actividades que te ofrecen los profesores se denominan de dos formas diferentes en Classroom: materiales y tareas. Los **materiales** y las **tareas** contienen actividades muy similares, tienen una diferencia importante:

- ❖ Cuando un profesor asigna **materiales**, sólo hay que abrirlos y hacer lo que se encuentra en las instrucciones.

- Cuando un profesor asigna **tareas** lugar, además de abrir ellos y haciendo lo que se encuentra en las instrucciones, **tienes que devolverlos**, de lo contrario, no se lleva a cabo la tarea; mira a continuación cómo hacerlo

Para **abrir un material o una tarea**, simplemente haz clic en él. Puedes hacer esto desde la pestaña Stream o la pestaña Materiales del curso, no cambia. Encuentra instrucciones que le dicen qué hacer y muy a menudo encuentra anexos que necesita leer, estudiar y completar... según las indicaciones de tus profesores.

Si **abre un material**, simplemente encontrará instrucciones y archivos adjuntos. Sigue las instrucciones, consulta los anexos y no tendrá que hacer nada más.

Haz tu tarea y devuélvela

Si **abres una tarea** haces lo mismo que se ve para el material: al final, sin embargo, **tienes que entregarlo**. Encontrarás dos claves **diferentes en función del tipo de tarea** que te hayas encomendado el profesor.

1. Si necesitas completar un documento de Google **en la tarea**, verá una pantalla como esta:

Para hacer su trabajo, en este ejemplo complete la tabla, haz clic a la derecha, en la columna 'Tu trabajo', arriba del icono del documento: el documento se abrirá en una nueva pestaña de Chrome. Cuando hayas completado el documento, no debes guardar (guardar tu mismo) y **no debes hacer clic en el botón azul Compartir**. En su lugar, debes **hacer clic en Entrega.**

Confirma que quieres entregar en el recuadro que aparece: de esta forma el profesor recibió tu tarea.

2. Sin embargo, si no hay documentos de Google para completar **en la tarea**, pero otros tipos de archivos adjuntos en los que trabajar, aparece una pantalla ligeramente diferente:

En este caso, después de haber realizado la tarea siguiendo las instrucciones, simplemente haz clic en Marcar como completada (con la siguiente confirmación), y la tarea es devuelta.

Agregar más archivos a la tarea

Puede suceder que necesites **agregar más archivos a la tarea asignada**. Por ejemplo, la foto de los ejercicios que hiciste en el libro. O tienes que hacer un nuevo documento para escribir un texto, y así sucesivamente. Para agregar un archivo, mire a la derecha en la columna 'Tu trabajo', y **haz clic en la opción Agregar o crear botón**. Al hacer clic aparece este menú:

Si necesitas agregar un archivo que ya ha creado (por ejemplo, la foto de los ejercicios, el archivo de audio con la ejecución de la pieza del instrumento, o cualquier otro archivo adjunto) haz clic en Archivo si tiene que cargarlo desde tu computadora o dispositivo móvil; de lo contrario, elige Google Drive si ya cargaste el archivo en tu unidad. También puedes crear nuevos archivos directamente desde aquí, eligiendo uno de los últimos 4 elementos. Puedes adjuntar varios archivos repitiendo la operación varias veces. Cuando hayas adjuntado lo que necesitas, luego haz clic en Entrega.

DESDE UN DISPOSITIVO MÓVIL

Entrar en en al Aula

Desde un teléfono inteligente o tableta, no uses el navegador (Chrome u otros): debes usar la aplicación Classroom. **Antes de** usar la aplicación, debes **agregar la cuenta de G Suite a tu dispositivo** desde la configuración; si lo necesitas, puedes seguir las instrucciones de la guía dedicada. Instala la aplicación Classroom desde Play Store o App Store. Cuando abras la aplicación, verifica que esté seleccionada la cuenta de G Suite y no tu cuenta personal de Gmail u otras cuentas; si lo necesitas, sigue las instrucciones de la guía dedicada.

Entrar al curso: materiales y tareas

Todo como desde una computadora, con la única diferencia de que los íconos para cambiar de Stream a Course work se encuentran en la parte inferior en lugar de en la parte superior.

Mira los materiales

No hay diferencia con la computadora.

Haz tu tarea y devuélvela

Todo según la computadora. La única diferencia es esta: para mostrar la columna **Tu trabajo**, que contiene los botones **Entrega** o **Marcar**como completada, debes hacer clic en el triángulo que ves a continuación. Después de hacer clic en él, verás todas las opciones en la columna.

Desde un dispositivo móvil, cuando haces clic en **agregar archivo adjunto**, tienes algunas opciones más: puedes tomar fotos o grabar videos directamente desde allí, sin tener que prepararlos primero. Así que **si tienes que adjuntar la foto de los ejercicios**, por ejemplo, puedes saltarte un paso a fotografiarlos **directamente desde dentro de la tarea**, eligiendo **Agregar archivo adjunto > Tomar foto.**

Guía básica de Google Aula para estudiantes

La interfaz de Google Classroom es simple. Los profesores pueden crear una página para cada clase y luego invitar a sus alumnos. A través de la plataforma, puedes enviar y programar mensajes a todos los estudiantes (o solo a un grupo).

Una de las funciones más útiles es la que te permite crear materiales educativos. Esto puede ayudarte con otras herramientas como documentos, presentaciones y hojas de cálculo. También tendrás a tu alcance una carpeta compartida en Google Drive.

1. Menú

Aquí encontrarás un calendario, una lista de tareas pendientes, tus clases y mucho más.

2. Tablón

Aquí es donde verá las comunicaciones entre estudiantes y profesores.

3. Trabajo en clase

Podrás crear materiales educativos, asignar tareas y hacer preguntas a la clase.

4. P as personas

Se guarda toda la información relacionada con los alumnos que forman parte de la clase. Puedes eliminar a un alumno de la clase virtual cuando desees.

5. Calificaciones

Con Google Classroom también puedes tomar nota de las tareas.

6. Configuración de la clase

Puedes cambiar la configuración de la clase y acceder fácilmente a otros servicios de Google.

7. Código de clase

Los estudiantes deben ingresar este código para unirse a la clase.

8. Tema

Puedes personalizar la interfaz de cada clase con una imagen de archivo o la suya propia.

9. Próxima fecha de entrega

Los estudiantes encontrarán aquí una lista de todas las tareas pendientes.

10. Publicaciones

Puedes compartir archivos, enlaces y tareas con la clase.

AULA DE GOOGLE PARA ESTUDIANTES

Cómo unirse y participar y los cuatro tipos de asignaciones

En esta sección, aprenderá a usar Google Classroom como estudiante. Para utilizar Google Classroom.

Lo primero que debes tener es una cuenta de Google. Así que dirígete a google.com e inicia sesión si ya tienes una cuenta, o crea una nueva. Una vez que hayas iniciado sesión o creado una cuenta, haz clic en Google Apps, desplázate hacia abajo y elige Google Classroom.

Bienvenido a tu lista de clases de Google Classroom. Aquí es donde verás todas las clases en las que se ha inscrito. Hay dos formas de unirse a una nueva clase. Primero, si tu professor teha dado un código de clase, haz clic en el signo 'más' y haz clic en 'Unirse a la clase'. Ingresa el código de clase que te ha proporcionado tu profesor. Si tu profesor te ha invitado por correo electrónico, verás una invitación para unirte a la clase. Se verá así con el nombre de la clase, el nombre de su maestro, el Avatar del maestro y dos opciones rechazar y unirse. Elige unirte.

Bienvenido a la pantalla de inicio de Google Classroom. Primero está tu 'corriente'. Aquí es donde aparecerán todos los anuncios y todas las tareas nuevas una vez que un maestro las haya publicado. En este momento, hay cuatro publicaciones y hay un anuncio. A la izquierda, ves los próximos eventos y las fechas de vencimiento. En la parte superior, verá tres pestañas "flujo". Lo que estamos viendo ahora, el trabajo en clase y la gente apuñalada, contendrá listas de maestros que están enseñando esta clase y también de sus compañeros de clase.

La mayor parte del tiempo trabajará desde la pestaña "Trabajo de clase", que contendrá publicaciones o tareas de su profesor. Los profesores pueden publicar cuatro tipos diferentes de tareas. El primer tipo es una tarea simple. El segundo tipo es una tarea de prueba. La tercera es una pregunta. Y finalmente, hay un material.

Ahora echemos un vistazo a cada tipo con más detalle. Si el profesor ha creado una asignación, lo más probable es contener las siguientes cosas. Primero, hay un nombre de la tarea en este momento, es solo una tarea. Si hay una fecha de vencimiento, la fecha de vencimiento aparecerá a la derecha. A continuación, hay una lista de instrucciones, una rúbrica y materiales de apoyo. Lo que voy a hacer como un estudiante es seguir las instrucciones de los maestros.

Mi primera instrucción es leer el artículo titulado«Transformando la educación en Minecraft». Ahora el artículo está aquí para leerlo, simplemente haz clic en él. Esto abrirá una nueva ventana, que puedes usar para leer el artículo. La segunda tarea es utilizar un documento titulado Reflexión personal para expresar mis pensamientos. El profesor también me ha proporcionado un documento para mi reflexión personal y el profesor también me ha proporcionado una rúbrica, que puedo usar para ver qué tipo de elección de palabras, gramática y estructura necesito usar para obtener el máximo número de puntos. Usaré esta rúbrica para escribir mi reflexión personal.

Para escribir una reflexión personal, haz clic en el archivo. Una vez que hayas hecho clic en el archivo, se abrirá la pestaña. Este es un documento de Google, que utilizará para escribir tu reflexión. Supongamos que terminé mi reflexión. Y estoy listo para entregar mi trabajo. Entonces, lo que voy a hacer es hacer clic en "entregar" y Google Classroom me advierte que si estoy listo para enviar mi tarea, haré clic en convertirla. Pero creo que hay una asignación más de mi maestro, así que no voy a convertir mi asignación. Por ahora, voy a volver a mis misiones y reconstrucción "grabar y enviar un breve video blog o un podcast sobre cómo utilizo los videojuegos con fines educativos". Para esta tarea, no tengo una plantilla, no tengo un archivo o un artículo para leer. De hecho, necesito crear una carga. Para hacer eso, haz clic en Ver tarea. Debido a que ya hemos completado nuestra reflexión, nuestra reflexión está aquí en nuestro trabajo, pero aún no hemos entregado nuestro trabajo, lo que significa que nuestro maestro no podrá verlo todavía. Porque aún nos queda un paso más.

Supongamos que he grabado mi podcast y ahora estoy listo para subir esto a Google Classroom. Para cargar archivos en Google Classroom, haz clic en Agregar o crear. Luego, elija dónde se almacenan sus archivos Google Drive o un enlace de Internet o archivos. En mi caso, tengo archivos en mi computadora. Entonces voy a hacer clic en archivos, seleccionar archivos de mi dispositivo y seleccionar los archivos que me gustaría cargar. En este caso, seleccionar los tres, hacer clic en abrir y luego subir. Google Drive tardará un par de segundos en cargar mis archivos en Google

Classroom. Ahora, una vez que haya terminado, volveré a la pantalla de Google Classroom.

Ahora tengo más archivos en mi trabajo, mi reflejo, mi archivo de audio, mi imagen y el bloque de video. La cantidad de archivos variará según las instrucciones de tu maestro, pero tienes que saber que puede enviar diferentes tipos de medios: archivos, archivos de imágenes e incluso archivos imagenes y videos. Una vez que esté listo para entregar su trabajo, haz clic en "entregar", Google Classroom te preguntará una vez más si deseas enviar estos archivos como respuesta. Si está seguro de "haz clic en entregar". Ahora, cuando nuestra tarea se haya entregado, es hora de que el docente vea tu tarea y le dé la calificación.

Después de que el profesor haya devuelto tu trabajo, han cambiado un par de cosas. Primero, le dieron una calificación final que se generó a partir de la rúbrica. Recuerda cómo vimos esta rúbrica antes de la tarea. Ahora que tu profesor ha marcado tu nivel para ver dónde llegaste en cada criterio, haz clic en expandir. El profesor también te ha dejado en un comentario privado. Una comunicación privada es un comunicado que solo tú puedes leer. Si desea responderle a su profesor, puedes hacerlo usando la función 'agregar comentario privado'.

Hemos analizado la tarea y cómo podemos enviar diferentes tipos de archivos para responder a la tarea de nuestro profesor. Nuestra tarea ahora está calificada. Así que pasemos a otro tipo de tarea, que es la tarea de prueba. Una vez que se hace clic en la asignación cuestionario, como de costumbre, verá una fecha de vencimiento, se consulta las instrucciones de los maestros, y que también verá un cuestionario, que es una forma Google. Para completar el cuestionario, haz clic en los Formularios de Google. Una vez que hagas clic en Formularios de Google, Google Classroom te llevará al cuestionario. Un cuestionario de Google puede contener diferentes tipos de preguntas. Los dos primeros son de opción múltiple. Nuestra tercera pregunta tiene casillas de verificación para que puedan ser más de una respuesta correcta. Nuestra pregunta final es una pregunta abierta, lo que significa que debe escribir su respuesta.

Una vez que hayas completado la prueba, asegúrate de hacer clic en el botón "Enviar". Ahora tu tarea se ha entregado y es hora de que tu profesor la califique y te la devuelva. Una vez que un docente haya calificado y devuelto su trabajo, verá su puntaje aquí mismo.

Sigamos adelante y veamos otro tipo de asignación, que es 'pregunta'. Este tipo de asignación por lo general contiene una pregunta y tal vez algunos materiales de apoyo. En este caso, un maestro ha establecido instrucciones para ver el videoclip del problema del carrito, que se adjunta a la pregunta, y luego escribir una respuesta a la pregunta «¿Qué haría yo en esta situación?» Imaginemos que vi el videoclip y estoy listo para responder la pregunta. Para responder a la pregunta, haz clic en Ver pregunta. Escribe tu respuesta aquí.

Una vez que su respuesta esté lista, haz clic en "entregar". Google Classroom le preguntará si estoy seguro de que quiero entregar porque no podré hacer cambios en mi respuesta. Una vez que he resuelto el nombre, estoy seguro y me voy a convertir en un maestro, como siempre me instruyó para responder a por lo menos dos de mis compañeros de clase. Es posible que hayas notado que una vez que haya enviado mi respuesta, ahora puedo ver los comentarios de mis compañeros de clase y responderles. Así que voy a hacer clic en ver los comentarios de los compañeros de clase y responderlos. Mi nombre es Ms three iPad three, y Ms. One iPad one ha publicado una respuesta. Para responder a tu compañero de clase, haz clic en "responder".

Mi comentario o respuesta ahora está grabado en su ms one iPad one. Esta es mi respuesta a mi compañero de clase, otros estudiantes podrían responder a tu respuesta. Así que asegúrate de consultar el tablero de discusión y tener una discusión productiva con tu compañero de clase.

Regresemos a la clase y echemos un vistazo al tipo final de tarea que es un material. A diferencia de la tarea de preguntas o cuestionarios para una tarea simple, el material no requiere tu presentación. En otras palabras, no necesita enviar nada en el material. En este caso, un maestro ha asignado un material y las instrucciones utilizan el material para revisar para la próxima prueba del lunes, y el material es un enlace a un videoclip de khan academy. Si haces clic en Ver material, lo único que puedes hacer es agregar un comentario de clase. No se requieren otras acciones además de ver el clip.

Veamos lo que has aprendido hoy. Hemos aprendido cómo unirnos a Google Classroom mediante el código de la clase o la invitación directa de su profesor. También analizamos cuatro tipos diferentes de asignación: asignación, asignación de prueba, pregunta y material. Además, también hemos aprendido a responder a cada tipo de tarea.

CAPÍTULO 5:
EXTENSIÓN Y APLICACIONES

Las 13 mejores extensiones de Google Chrome imprescindibles para profesores

En esta sección, voy a mostrarles cuales 13 extensiones de Google Chrome deben tener para profesores. La combinación correcta de extensiones de Google Chrome puede ayudarte a organizar los materiales, puede ayudarte a brindar instrucción de manera más efectiva, además, también puede hacer que lo que presentas a los estudiantes sea más divertido y atractivo. Ya sea para grabar tutoriales en video de captura de pantalla para estudiantes, dibujar y hacer anotaciones directamente en la pantalla de la computadora que está proyectando, enviar sitios web a las computadoras de los estudiantes, traducir automáticamente páginas web a otros idiomas o ayudarte a guardar y organizar fácilmente páginas web, imágenes y archivos en el lugar correcto. Las extensiones de Google Chrome encenderán su navegador de Internet y harán su vida como profesor un poco más fácil.

Primero, es importante tener en cuenta que para usar las extensiones de Google Chrome, debe usar el navegador de Internet Google Chrome. Todas las extensiones que voy a mostrarte se pueden encontrar en la tienda de Google Chrome y puedes descargarlas gratis. Así que vayamos a la tienda de Google Chrome para comprobarlo. Como verás, hay toneladas de diferentes extensiones de Google Chrome que puedes agregar para encender tu navegador y personalizarlo y prácticamente de la forma que desees; puedes ver aquí en mi navegador Chrome que ya agregué un montón de diferentes extensiones de Chrome. Una vez que los haya instalado. Puedes arrastrarlos y soltarlos donde desees cambiar el orden. Y si deseas eliminar una extensión que agregaste, simplemente haz clic derecho y presiona Eliminar. De acuerdo, hay toneladas de diferentes extensiones de Chrome.

Y solo tengo tiempo aquí para concentrarme en las extensiones de Chrome más impactantes que puedes tener en tu vida como profesor.

1. Screencastify

La primera y creo que la extensión de Google Chrome más importante que debes tener es Screencastify. Por ello, Screencastify te permite crear fácilmente tutoriales en video para tus estudiantes que luego puedes publicar en tu aula digital, como Google Classroom. Una vez que hayas creado un video tutorial, los estudiantes pueden verlos a su propio ritmo, pueden ver videos fuera de la clase y les prometo que una vez que comiences a usarlo, transformará por completo la forma en que enseñas.

Para esta primera extensión, voy a recorrer todo el proceso de cómo instalarla en tu navegador. Cuando esté listo para agregar la extensión, haz clic en Agregar a Chrome, haz clic en Agregar extensión. Y en este caso con Screencastify, se le pedirá que configures rápidamente una cuenta la primera vez que la uses. Así que vamos a decir que estoy en un programa como Book Creator, y quiero enseñar a mis estudiantes cómo van a utilizarlo. Todo lo que hago es subir a la extensión Screencastify, haz clic en ella, luego haz clic en grabar, y comenzará a grabar una captura de pantalla de lo que estoy haciendo en la pantalla, así como mi voz e incluso un video de mí mismo si elijo esa opción. Una vez que esté listo para detener el video, haz clic en la extensión nuevamente y luego haz clic en detener. Y allí se le ofrecerán un montón de opciones diferentes. Si deseas compartir el video en Google Classroom directamente, en un canal de YouTube que hayas creado o en tu Google Drive. Puedes hacer cualquiera de esos con tu video.

2. TabTijeras

La siguiente extensión que necesita se llama tijeras de pestañas. Una vez que tengas instaladas las tijeras de pestañas, te permitirá dividir uniformemente dos pestañas que tiene en su navegador, para que ambas estén visibles en la pantalla. Tab Scissors puede ser increíblemente útil si estás tratando de ingresar notas en tu libro de calificaciones de tareas en una página separada en Google Classroom, o si está tratando de ingresar nombres en un sitio web de una lista de clases que ha sacado de una Hojas de Google. Para volver a juntar esas pestañas, querrá obtener una tercera extensión llamada pegamento de pestañas.

3. Tab Glue

Una vez que hayas instalado el programa, todo lo que tienes que hacer es dar clic en esa extensión y pegará las dos pestañas que acabas de separar.

4. Web Paint

Otra extensión esencial de Google Chrome se llama Web Paint. Si proyectas mucho la pantalla de tu computadora en clase, esta cambiará absolutamente tu vida. Digamos que está proyectando un sitio web como Newsela y deseas enfatizar el título de un artículo, simplemente haz clic en el icono de pintura web, haz clic en la herramienta de dibujo. Puedes cambiar el tamaño y el color y luego puedes dibujar libremente en toda la página web que está proyectando para los estudiantes. Convierte cada página web que proyectas en algo totalmente personalizable para que escribas como quieras.

Hay otras herramientas interesantes como Relleno de color, puedes dibujar un cuadro alrededor del título de este artículo y luego rellenar el resto del fondo para enfatizar realmente el título del artículo para los estudiantes. La pintura web es increíble. Es una herramienta que uso casi a diario ahora en mis clases.

5. Compartir en el aula

La siguiente extensión que les mostraré compartir en el aula es una extensión que uso a diario. Y si es un usuario de Google Classroom, es una extensión que debes tener. Para que la extensión de compartir en el aula funcione, los estudiantes también deben tener esa extensión instalada en sus navegadores. Una vez que lo tengan instalado. Puedes enviarles sitios web en cualquier momento durante la clase, ni siquiera necesitan iniciar sesión en su Google Classroom.

Entonces, digamos que quiero compartir este artículo con mis estudiantes sobre el Gran Parche de Basura del Pacífico. Todo lo que tengo que hacer es hacer clic en el icono Compartir en el aula y luego hacer clic en el botón. Y ese sitio web aparecerá inmediatamente en las computadoras de los estudiantes de mi clase. En lugar de tener que llamar la atención de todos y decir, «Ey, quiero que todos vayan a esta otra página web». Todo lo que hago ahora es presionar a los estudiantes y ese sitio web aparece para toda mi clase. Realmente es un cambio de juego.

Además de enviar una tarea a los estudiantes, verás que también puedes tomar esa página web y convertirla en una tarea, convertirla en una pregunta o un recurso que va a publicar en Google Classroom.

6. Google Keep

Las siguientes dos extensiones me ayudaron a organizar mis materiales y optimizar mi flujo de trabajo. Soy un usuario de Google Keep, utilizo Google Keep como un sistema de notas adhesivas en línea, en lugar de una lista de tareas en papel para realizar un seguimiento de todas las cosas diferentes que debo hacer. Google Keep es genial, porque también puedes compartirlo con otras personas como tus alumnos. Y una forma de utilizarlo en clase es hacer una lista colaborativa de diferentes recursos sobre un tema.

Entonces, digamos que tienes una nota adhesiva compartida de Google Keep y encuentras un recurso que te gusta y deseas agregar a una lista, simplemente haz clic en la extensión de Google Keep. Y luego, si lo deseas, puedes agregar un título y una etiqueta si está creando una nueva. Y verá cuando regreses a Google Keep que ahora tienes una etiqueta con ese recurso específico.

7. Guardar en Google Drive

Para propósitos similares, también recomiendo que obtengas la extensión 'Guardar en unidad'. Una vez que hayas instalado la extensión de Google Drive, cualquier cosa en la que haz clic con el botón derecho se puede agregar automáticamente a su Google Drive. Entonces, digamos que encuentras una imagen que te gusta, en lugar de descargarla a tu computadora y luego volver a cargarla en su Google Drive, ahora puedes guardar esa imagen directamente en tu carpeta de Google Drive para agilizar tu flujo de trabajo y hacer tu vida más sencilla un poco más fácil. Una vez que lo hayas guardado, verá que puedes cambiar el destino de tu ubicación en Google Drive. Y también puedes cambiar la configuración predeterminada si deseas que todo vaya constantemente en el mismo lugar.

8. Captura de pantalla de página completa con un clic

A continuación, te recomiendo que obtengas la extensión de captura de pantalla. Entonces, digamos que has encontrado un recurso que deseas o estás mirando el proyecto de un estudiante y deseas hacer una captura de pantalla para cargarlo en el aula de Google o en el sitio web de una clase. Todo lo que necesitas hacer es hacer clic en la captura de pantalla y producirá una captura de pantalla instantánea de esa página. Verás en la parte inferior que también hay diferentes herramientas de anotación si deseas modificarlo, y luego puedes hacer clic en descargar para abrir la captura de pantalla.

9. Traductor de google

A continuación, te recomiendo que obtengas la extensión Google Translate. Traductor Google es muy potente, y te permitirá auto-traducir todo lo que está en frente de la pantalla. Entonces, digamos que necesito traducir este sitio web a otro idioma para uno de mis estudiantes, todo lo que necesito hacer es ir a la extensión Google Translate, hacer clic en traducir esta página, seleccionar un idioma al que quiero traducir. Y allí verás que la página web ahora está completamente traducida al español.

Esto también se aplica a Google Docs. Así que si tienes tiene un documento que necesitas traducir rápidamente, y hay que compartirlo con las familias o estudiantes, lo mismo, haz clic en Google Translate, seleccionar un idioma y verá que ha sido auto-traducido. Ahora, por supuesto, la traducción no es 100% perfecta, pero es una gran opción si necesitas mejorar tu comunicación con estudiantes y familias que hablan otro idioma.

10. Calendario de Google

A continuación, para mi propia organización personal y cordura, me gusta tener la extensión de Google Calendar en mi navegador. Una vez que hayas agregado la extensión, verás que indica cuánto tiempo tienes hasta tu próximo evento programado. También puedes hacer clic en la extensión del calendario para ver tu horario general del día. Me parece realmente útil echar un vistazo rápido a lo que estoy haciendo sin tener que abrir mi calendario en una pestaña separada.

11. PDF pequeño

A continuación, les mostraré un pequeño PDF y este podría volar tu mente un poco. Pequeño PDF es una extensión de Google que te permitirá auto-convertir cualquier documento de un formato a otro. Digamos que tienes un PDF y solo deseas convertirlo rápidamente en un documento de Word. Puedes usar un PDF pequeño para hacer exactamente eso. Entonces, la forma en que funciona es que hace clic en un PDF pequeño, elige el tipo de archivo que desea convertir hacia y desde, luego verás que me lleva a una página web donde voy a arrastrar el archivo que deseas convertir, haz clic en 'Convertir a Word', convertirá tu documento y ahora tengo un documento editable de un documento que anteriormente no podía editar. También puede ir al revés y convertir un documento de Word en un PDF, o elegir entre una variedad de otros tipos de formatos.

12. Bitmoji

Las dos últimas extensiones de Google Chrome que les voy a mostrar en realidad solo se trata de agregar un poco más de factor de alegría a sus clases. La primera es la extensión bitmoji. Ahora es importante mencionar que necesitas configurar bitmoji en iOS o Android para poder usarlo. Una vez que se hayas registrado y creado una cuenta de bitmoji, puedes hacer clic en la extensión y luego elegir entre una amplia variedad de avatares de ti mismo haciendo cosas diferentes y diciendo cosas diferentes que puedes colocar en Presentaciones de Google o en correos electrónicos o documentos para hacer son un poco más divertidos y atractivos además de bitmoji.

13. Giphy

También me gustó mucho usar la extensión Giphy para Chrome. Con Giphy, puedes seleccionar entre una amplia gama de diferentes gifs animados y, una vez que encuentres uno que te guste, todo lo que tienes que hacer es arrastrarlo y soltarlo en una diapositiva o un documento. Nuevamente, solo para que sea un poco más divertido y atractivo para los estudiantes.

Claramente, hay una enorme cantidad de extensiones de Google Chrome. Pero creo que estos 13 son los más importantes para los maestros en términos de ayudartea agilizar tu flujo de trabajo, presentar información de manera más efectiva para los estudiantes y también agregar un poco de factor de alegría al trabajo que presenta a tu clase. Estoy seguro de que muchos tienen otras sugerencias sobre las increíbles extensiones de Google Chrome para profesores.

Las 12 mejores aplicaciones de Google Classroom

Google Classroom se ha convertido en una herramienta imprescindible para los profesores. Este recurso gratuito permite a los educadores asignar trabajos, realizar un seguimiento del progreso y comunicarse con los estudiantes y los padres en línea. Mejora aún más tu experiencia en Google Classroom con estas aplicaciones y sitios web, todos los cuales se integran a la perfección con su aula en línea. La mayoría son completamente gratis; algunas ofrecen opciones de pago, pero sus versiones gratuitas tienen muchas funciones gratuitas fantásticas que vale la pena explorar.

1. CK-12

No creerás la increíble cantidad de recursos gratuitos disponibles en CK-12. Cada materia, cada grado... todo está cubierto en videos, ejercicios, lecciones e incluso libros de texto completos. Es muy fácil asignar cualquiera de estos elementos en Google Classroom, y la finalización y las calificaciones se registran en su libro de calificaciones en línea. (Web)

2. Edpuzzle

Convierte cualquier video en cualquier lugar en una lección interactiva, o incluso carga el tuyo. Agrega preguntas, audio o notas para que los estudiantes puedan ver y aprender a su propio ritmo. Las funciones de seguimiento les permite controlar sus progresos y comprensión, e integrarse fácilmente con Google Classroom. El sólido plan gratuito incluye almacenamiento de hasta 20 videos a la vez. (Web, iOS y Android)

3. Explica todo

Explica todo es una aplicación de pizarra, y se puede usar como si se tratara de una pizarra digital interactiva en el aula. Aún mejor, te permite registrar tus interacciones y compartirlas a través de Google Classroom para que los estudiantes las vean más tarde. La versión gratuita tiene algunas limitaciones, pero ofrece muchas funciones interesantes; hay planes de educación premium disponibles. (Web, iOS y Android)

4. Flipgrid

Con Flipgrid, los estudiantes graban videos cortos para responder a los temas que les asignan. Esta es una aplicación especialmente interesante para los estudiantes que dudan en hablar en vivo en las llamadas de Zoom; les da a todos la oportunidad de ser escuchados. Es fácil compartir sus cuadrículas y asignaciones con Google Classroom. (Web, iOS y Android)

5. Google Cast for Education

Esta simple extensión de Chrome hace que sea muy fácil compartir la pantalla con cualquier persona. En un salón de clases (en persona o virtual), los estudiantes comparten su pantalla con el maestro y el maestro la comparte con la clase mediante un proyector o mediante Google Classroom. Es simple, gratis y una necesidad para todos los usuarios. (Web)

6. Khan Academy

Muchos profesores ya están familiarizados con la increíblemente amplia gama de recursos gratuitos de aprendizaje en línea de Khan Academy. Cubren todas las materias y niveles de grado, y brindan a los estudiantes la práctica adicional que necesitan para dominar conceptos importantes. Crea e integra clases usando sus listas de Google Classroom y estará listo para asignar contenido. (Web, iOS y Android)

7. Escucha

Cada día, Listenwise publica un nuevo podcast gratuito de eventos actuales que puede compartir con sus estudiantes. Estas breves lecciones de audio son ideales para reuniones matutinas o para iniciar debates generales sobre eventos actuales. Listenwise Premium ofrece una gran biblioteca de podcasts con lecciones, cuestionarios y transcripciones interactivas, actualmente gratis para probar durante 90 días. (Web)

8. Quizizz

Quizizz es una herramienta ingeniosa para ayudar a los estudiantes a revisar lo que están aprendiendo en clase. Utiliza uno de los miles de cuestionarios que ya están disponibles o cree uno propio. Organice juegos de preguntas en vivo en línea en clase o asígnelos como tarea con Google Classroom. Personaliza cada tarea para indicar cuántas veces un alumno puede intentar cada pregunta y si ves las respuestas correctas cuando hayas terminado:

retroalimentación instantánea que hace que el aprendizaje sea más significativo. (Web, iOS y Android)

9. Quizlet

Esta es una de las aplicaciones de tarjetas de memoria flash en línea más populares y es completamente gratuita. Encuentra las flashcards que necesitas en su extensa biblioteca o crea las tuyas propias para apoyar cualquier tipo de lección. Comparta las flashcards en Google Classroom para brindarles a los estudiantes acceso instantáneo a estas herramientas de práctica en la escuela o en casa. (Web, iOS y Android)

10. Science Buddies

Este sitio es el mejor amigo de todo profesor de ciencias. Está repleto de videos, planes de lecciones y experimentos gratuitos, todos se pueden buscar por nivel de grado y materia. Esta también es una excelente opción durante la temporada de ferias de ciencias, con abundantes recursos de métodos científicos, herramientas de planificación de ferias de ciencias y un enorme depósito de ideas de proyectos. Cuando usas Science Buddies con Google Classroom, también obtienes acceso a pruebas y evaluaciones adicionales. (Web)

11. Wakelet

Piensa en Wakelet como una herramienta colaborativa para organizar y compartir información. Úsalo para crear y compartir lecciones con tus alumnos mediante la recopilación de medios en un solo lugar, con sus propias notas y explicaciones. Y aun mejor, haz que tus estudiantes lo utilicen para crear presentaciones, informes de libros, boletines informativos y más directamente en Google Classroom. (Web, iOS y Android)

12. Banco de trabajo

Workbench es una colección de lecciones y videos que se pueden compartir sobre todo tipo de temas. Busca y asigna lecciones existentes, o crea las tuyas propias para una experiencia personalizada. Inserta videos, proporciona instrucciones e incluso diseña proyectos completos para que los estudiantes los completen con los recursos de este sitio gratuito. (Web)

CAPÍTULO 6: OTRAS COSAS INCREÍBLES SOBRE EL AULA DE GOOGLE

Diez razones por las que debería utilizar Google Classroom

Si pudiéramos ofrecer a los maestros y profesores algo que les ahorraría tiempo, ahorraría dinero en la escuela, se comunicaría mejor con los estudiantes y los padres, ayudaría a los estudiantes con dificultades e impactaría el entorno de aprendizaje de los estudiantes... ¿Podrías considerar cantarlo? Supongo que lo harían. Si has estado usando Google Classroom durante los últimos años, probablemente ya sepas por qué es bueno usarlo. Pero si es nuevo para ti, probablemente deses saber las razones por las que estes cambio es adecuado para los estudiantes.

A continuación, se incluyen algunas cosas a considerar: **Google Classroom es fácil de usar**. En comparación con otros LMS (sistemas de gestión de aprendizaje) o "sistemas de gestión de aprendizaje" que han sido populares en la última década, Google Classroom es increíblemente simple. Crear un aula nueva no requiere mucho tiempo ni experiencia. Nuestro equipo técnico se entrenó durante una hora y todos teníamos un aula preparada y funcionando al final de la sesión.

1. **Google Classroom te ayuda a comunicarte de manera más eficiente.** Ingresa las direcciones de correo electrónico de los estudiantes solo una vez y se realiza la comunicación en el aula. Simplemente ingresando al estudiante en el aula, el docente tiene un grupo de correo electrónico, un grupo de discusión y un Calendario de Google creado automáticamente. Además, es fácil agregar y quitar estudiantes de la clase si es necesario.

2. **Google Classroom lo ayuda a comunicarse de manera más efectiva.** Probablemente más importantes que ser fáciles de usar y eficientes, las herramientas de comunicación también son muy efectivas. Debido a que todo está basado en la nube, los estudiantes ya no "pierden" tareas. Si un estudiante está ausente, la comunicación es perfecta. El mes pasado, Google Aula añadió una matriz característica de notificación para mantener a los padres informados de lo que está pasando en el "aula".

3. **Google Classroom es más rentable y mejor para el medio ambiente.** Personalmente, no estoy completamente "vendido" por el aprendizaje sin

papel, especialmente para los estudiantes más jóvenes. Pero veo una ventaja real en hacer que las escuelas sean más rentables cuando se trata de copiar e imprimir. Si cada estudiante tiene un dispositivo que se conecta a Internet, cada hoja de papel que guardamos solo hace que la escuela sea más eficiente y responsable con el medio ambiente.

4. **Así es como los estudiantes continuarán aprendiendo en el futuro.** En el ámbito universitario ya no se espera que los estudiantes de tercer año impriman sus ensayos de cinco páginas. Como maestros de K-12, debemos tomar nota y preparar a nuestros estudiantes para el mundo en el que vivirán.

5. **Es mejor para estudiantes con dificultades...** siempre que les ayuda a administrar el dispositivo. (El dispositivo en sí puede ser una distracción a veces, por lo que es necesario enseñar a administrar). La razón por la que Google Classroom es mejor es por la ventaja organizativa que les brinda. Las asignaciones nunca se pierden y cada clase ya está organizada por el profesor. Sin embargo, para estos estudiantes, se debe enseñar a navegar por esto. Aunque los estudiantes sean nativos digitales, eso no significa que comprendan cómo los adultos organizan su mundo para ayudarlos a aprender.

6. **Con Google Classroom, la colaboración es más fácil fuera de la escuela (es decir, Flipped Classroom).** Una vez más, está basado en la nube y es accesible

desde cualquier lugar con conexión. Los estudiantes pueden compartir asignaciones y trabajar juntos desde casa para completarlas. La colaboración no se limita a trabajar en grupo con otros compañeros. Un docente puede darle la vuelta al aula compartiendo un video para que se pueda ver más tarde, de esta forma se puede preparar para el cuestionario del día siguiente. Las posibilidades son infinitas.

7. **La planificación del maestro es fácil y el tiempo inicial vale la pena.** Más funciones nuevas en Google Classroom permiten a los profesores programar tareas en el futuro. Las asignaciones designadas podrían programarse para realizarse en vivo un lunes y luego cerrarse el viernes. Si un maestro tiene una ausencia prolongada, el maestro puede programar tareas. Google Classroom también se puede utilizar de un semestre a otro y de un año a otro. Sería terrible para un maestro simplemente copiar y pegar un Google Classroom para el siguiente grupo de estudiantes, pero ahorra tiempo ya que te permite tener ciertas cosas ya establecidas (horario de clases, clasificación de expectativas, etc.)

8. **Al incorporar formularios, la retroalimentación es instantánea y utilizable.** Uno de mis maestros pedía a los estudiantes que completaran un cuestionario de opción múltiple mientras veían el video. Esto aumenta el compromiso y la responsabilidad, pero también permite que el docente vea los resultados al final del video. De esta manera, puede volver a cubrir

el material si los estudiantes tuvieron dificultades para responder con las respuestas correctas.

9. **Las mejoras y actualizaciones son una constante.** Este es, con mucho, uno de los mejores medios de Google Classroom para mí. Si es necesario agregar o arreglar algo, Google realmente escucha y responde. Esto también significa que los profesores tendrán que seguir aprendiendo mientras lo utilizan... que tampoco esta mal!

Estoy seguro de que Google Classroom ofrece más beneficios, pero estas son diez excelentes razones por las que vale la pena analizarlas más de cerca.

50 cosas que puedes hacer con Google Classroom

1. Hacer anuncios de clase
2. Compartir recursos
3. Varios archivos en una tarea
4. Crear una lección
5. Ver fácilmente la entrega de los estudiantes
6. Dejar de usar papel
7. Simplificar el proceso de entrega
8. Proteger la privacidad
9. Reducir las trampas

10. Colaboración en el aula
11. Creear una debates
12. Organizar las asignaciones con fechas límite
13. Comentarios antes de que los estudiantes envíen
14. Enviar un correo electrónico a los estudiantes
15. Notificar a los estudiantes que podrian necesitar ayuda
16. Preguntas y respuestas sobre las asignaciones
17. Crear una lista de reproducción ad hoc
18. Comentarios por correo electrónico
19. Crear carpetas
20. 20 Vincular directamente al trabajo del estudiante
21. Recopilar datos
22. Compartir con varias clases
23. Tomar de notas en conjunto
24. Mostrar el trabajo del estudiante
25. Un estudiante Una diapositiva
26. Dirigir las llamadas telefónicas de los padres
27. Encuestas
28. Compartir un documento con la clase

29. 29 Saber quién edita un documento colaborativo
30. Enlazar a un sitio web
31. Ayudar fuera del horario de atención
32. Comentarios grupales
33. Distribuir notas
34. Compartir el aprendizaje informal
35. Enviar un correo electrónico al maestro
36. Proyectos de los estudiantes
37. Eliminar los trabajos de Schlepping en casa
38. Tener un lugar para todos los Archivos
39. Documentar el trabajo digital
40. Los estudiantes crean en Google Docs
41. Identificar claramente el trabajo de los estudiantes
42. Ver asignaciones
43. Horas de oficina virtual
44. Colaborar con compañeros (PLC)
45. Reuniones virtuales de profesores
46. Optimización de la asesoría
47. Ver a los estudiantes hacer la tarea

48. Observar otro salón de clase
49. Compartir muestras de los alumnos
50. Ofrecer opciones

Ventajas y limitaciones de Google Classroom

Beneficios / ventajas de Google Chrome y Google Classroom

1. **Vista única del trabajo de los estudiantes:** para ayudar a los educadores a realizar un seguimiento del progreso individual de los estudiantes, hemos creado una página en Classroom dedicada a cada estudiante que muestra todo su trabajo en una clase. Con esta nueva vista, los profesores y los estudiantes pueden ver el estado de cada tarea y usar filtros para ver las asignaciones asignadas, faltantes o devueltas y calificadas. Los maestros y los estudiantes pueden usar esta información para tomar decisiones de aprendizaje personalizadas que ayuden a los estudiantes a establecer metas y desarrollar habilidades que les servirán en el futuro.

2. **Reorganizar las clases:** los educadores ahora pueden ordenar sus clases según el horario diario, las prioridades de la carga de trabajo o lo que les ayude a mantenerse organizados durante todo el año escolar. Y los estudiantes también pueden usar esta función. "Para los educadores y los estudiantes, la organización es importante, y poder reorganizar las

tarjetas de clase nos permite mantener nuestras clases organizadas de una manera simple y personalizada", dice Ross Berman, maestro de matemáticas de séptimo y octavo grado «Los estudiantes pueden cambiar de clase para que lo primero que vean sea la clase que saben que tendrán trabajo que hacer».

3. **Decimal de clasificación:** A medida que los maestros saben, la clasificación es a menudo más complicado que un valor de punto simple. Para ser lo más precisos posible con su evaluación, los educadores ahora pueden usar puntos decimales al calificar tareas en Google Classroom.

4. **Transferir la propiedad de la clase:** Las cosas pueden cambiar mucho durante el verano, incluido quién enseña qué clase. Los administradores y profesores ahora pueden transferir la propiedad de las clases en Google Classroom a otros profesores, sin tener que rehacer la clase. El nuevo propietario de la clase puede ponerse al día rápidamente con una vista completa del trabajo y los recursos de los alumnos anteriores en Drive.

5. **Agregar una imagen de perfil desde un dispositivo móvil:** los estudiantes de hoy acumulan muchas horas de uso en sus teléfonos. Pronto, los estudiantes podrán realizar cambios en su perfil móvil en Classroom directamente desde sus dispositivos móviles, incluido el cambio de su foto de perfil desde

la aplicación móvil Google Classroom. ¡Prepara las selfies!

6. **Administrar clases con School Directory Sync:** Google School Directory Sync ahora admite la sincronización de las clases de Google Classroom desde el sistema de administración de información de los estudiantes mediante archivos CSV de IMS OneRoster. Los administradores pueden ahorrar tiempo a los profesores y estudiantes al administrar la configuración de la clase antes de que suene la campana de la escuela.

7. **Las integraciones nueva aula:** las aplicaciones que se integran con el Aula proporcionan una experiencia perfecta para los educadores y les permite fácilmente compartir información entre el aula y otras herramientas que toplace de like.welcome nuevas aplicaciones a la #withClassroom familia: Quizizz, Edcite, Kami, y muy pronto, Code.org.

8. **Muestre el código de la clase:** unirse a las clases de Google Classroom es más fácil que nunca gracias a esta nueva actualización. Los profesores ahora pueden mostrar su código de clase en pantalla completa para que los estudiantes puedan unirse rápidamente a nuevas clases.

9. **¡Una vista previa! Importe las puntuaciones de las pruebas de autoevaluación en Google Forms a Classroom:** el uso de pruebas de autoevaluación en Google Forms permite a los educadores evaluar la

comprensión de los estudiantes de un tema en tiempo real. Pronto, los profesores podrán importar los resultados de las pruebas directamente a Google Classroom.

10. **Agregue comentarios a la puntuación de la prueba pregunta por pregunta:** más allá de las puntuaciones de la prueba, la retroalimentación significativa puede mejorar el aprendizaje.

Ventajas

Su funcionamiento es muy sencillo e intuitivo, y de hecho esta es la clave de su éxito. No es tan completo como otras plataformas de aprendizaje, pero cualquier profesor lo usa con facilidad con una formación mínima. De hecho, toda la comunicación online con los alumnos se realiza con esta herramienta. Ya no es necesario utilizar el correo electrónico y mucho menos WhatsApp o aplicaciones de usuario inseguras. Así, el profesor puede enviar notificaciones a su clase (oa un grupo específico) reemplazando la "agenda" del papel y permitiendo que los niños interactúen.

También te permite **hacer preguntas de seguimiento**, con la ventaja de tener instantáneamente las respuestas individuales de cada alumno, y también el resultado general. Y por supuesto, también **ofrece la posibilidad de enviar tareas** y así evitar hacer fotocopias para todos. Con un simple clic, cada uno tiene su copia del trabajo, para realizarlo, desde cualquier lugar (colegio, casa), en cualquier momento, y desde cualquier dispositivo (móvil, tableta, portátil o pc de cualquier marca y modelo).

En general, **ahorra papeleo administrativo** y permite una mejor organización además de trabajar con texto, videos, imágenes, ecuaciones, mapas mentales, pentagramas y cualquier producto que se pueda crear digitalmente.

Desventajas / Limitaciones

Realmente no hay ningún desafío urgente con Google Classroom. A cambio, **requiere que cada profesor y alumno tenga una cuenta "Google"**, lo que genera cierta preocupación enalgunas familias, en mi opinión infundada porque para las cuentas de Educación las condiciones de privacidad de Google son muy estrictas.

CAPÍTULO 7:
CONSEJOS Y TRUCOS PARA EL AULA DE GOOGLE

Tres consejos para organizar tu clase de Google:

En esta sección, veremos cómo mantener su Google Classroom agradable y organizado. Hay tres estrategias básicas que podemos usar para asegurarnos de que nuestro Google Classroom no se ensucie. Y estan:

1. Organizando por temas,
2. Reutilizar publicaciones y;
3. Archivar y eliminar aulas que ya no sabemos que necesitan.

¿Por qué no miramos cada una de estas estrategias una a la vez, y vamos a empezar con los temas?

1. Temas

Los temas son probablemente la forma más fácil de asegurarse de que el contenido que publica en Google

Classroom no se salga de control y sea de fácil acceso para ti y tus alumnos. Para utilizar temas para organizar su aula de Google, vaya al trabajo de clase, haz clic en 'Crear' y haz clic en el tema.

Antes de crear cualquier tema, piensa en cómo le gustaría compartimentar todo lo que has publicado en su Google Classroom. Es posible que tengas un montón de tareas, un montón de preguntas, un montón de materiales, etc. Piensa en cuáles son los temas en los que pueden caer todas tus publicaciones. Los tutores normalmente compartimentan su contenido por unidades o por tipo de publicaciones.

Permítanme demostrar primero cómo podemos clasificar nuestra publicación por unidades. Entonces, para hacer eso, crearemos tres unidades que estoy enseñando este semestre. Vamos a crear la unidad uno, crearemos otras unidades; la unidad dos y la unidad tres. Es posible que hayas notado que una vez que he creado esas unidades, aparecen a la izquierda de mi pantalla como una tabla de contenido porque tengo algunas publicaciones que se han generado antes de que ahora pueda intentar ordenarlas. Entonces sé que la asignación uno pertenece a la unidad uno. Entonces, lo que haré es simplemente tomarlo y arrastrarlo a la unidad uno. Inmediatamente, la tarea uno desaparecerá de mis publicaciones y aparecerá en la unidad uno. Haré lo mismo con otras publicaciones. Mi primer examen pertenece a la unidad tres. Mi pregunta sobre la creatividad pertenece a la Unidad Dos. Las indicaciones de mi ensayo pertenecen a la unidad tres y mi tarea dos pertenece a la unidad dos. Creo que empezamos a ver cómo nuestro Google Classroom puede verse mucho más organizado.

Cuando comenzamos a usar temas, hay un par de cosas que puedes hacer cuando se trata de editar los temas. Lo primero es cambiar el nombre, y una vez que hayas configurado un nombre, puedes cambiarle el nombre más adelante, puedes moverlos hacia arriba y hacia abajo o arrastrarlos desde la vista de temas antiguos. Una cosa importante para recordar por qué eliminar en un tema es que cuando elimina un tema, las publicaciones que pertenecen a este tema no se eliminarán. Lo que hice ahora: eliminé la unidad tres, que tenía indicaciones de ensayo y mi primera tarea de prueba, pero simplemente se movieron a un tema no asignado. Así que esta es una forma de organizar todo su contenido organizándolo por unidades.

Lo que también puedes hacer es organizar todo su contenido de acuerdo con el tipo de publicación. Google Classroom te permite crear cuatro tipos diferentes de cuestionarios de tareas, preguntas de tareas y materiales. Y estos podrían ser tus temas. Entonces, ¿por qué no seguimos adelante y tratamos de organizarnos de esta manera? Nuestro primer tema será la asignación. Nuestro segundo tema será la asignación de pruebas. Nuestro tercer tema será la cuestión. Y finalmente, nuestro cuarto tema será la asignación de material. Pasaremos al material de la tarea, pasaremos al material y así sucesivamente. Hay una cosa más que debo señalar es que puedes asignar tus publicaciones a temas mientras los creas para hacer eso, mientras estás creando, digamos una pregunta aquí, puedes seleccionar a qué tema se dirigirá esta publicación en particular ser asignado. Esta es una pregunta que planteé. Entonces, esto se asignará a una pregunta una vez que publiques esta pregunta, automáticamente pasará al tema de la pregunta. Estas son solo dos formas de categorizar tus publicaciones. Puedes idear tu propio método, pero esto es lo que yo personalmente hago, ya sea organizando por unidades o por tipo de asignaciones.

2. Reutilizar publicaciones

Otra cosa que puedes hacer para ayudarte a mantener su Google Classroom organizado es reutilizar las publicaciones. Creo que es más fácil demostrar cómo se hace. Entonces, digamos que esta es mi segunda aula de Google que no tiene nada ni trabajo en clase. Entonces, en lugar de crear una tarea desde cero, lo que puedo hacer es reutilizar publicaciones generadas en otro Google Classroom.

Déjame demostrarte lo que quiero decir. Si voy a crear y hago clic en reutilizar publicaciones, usamos publicación con la primera pregunta, de acuerdo, qué clase me gustaría usar una publicación de esta es la segunda clase de Google y me gustaría reutilizar publicaciones de mi primera clase de Google. Así que esto me llevará a mi primer aula de Google y puedo seleccionar una publicación que me gustaría reutilizar en mi segundo aula de Google. Entonces, en mi caso, me gustaría reutilizar la asignación. Primero, asegúrate de usar la política Crear nuevas copias para todos los archivos adjuntos para que los archivos adjuntos no se compartan entre dos grupos de estudiantes. Cuando hago clic en reutilizar ahora la tarea, una que se generó originalmente y mi primera clase de Google apareció en mi segunda clase de Google, por lo que esta es una manera realmente agradable de mantenerla organizada. En lugar de crear una nueva publicación una y otra vez, la función de reutilización de publicaciones te permite reciclar publicaciones que se han generado antes para las aulas actuales.

3. Archivar y eliminar aulas

Nuestra estrategia final para ayudarte a mantener tu Google Classroom ordenado y organizado es archivar y eliminar aulas que ya no enseña. Al final del año escolar, una gran cantidad de maestros se acercó a mí con la misma pregunta, ¿cómo eliminar Google aulas que no hacemos ninguna enseñar más? Les enseñamos el año pasado. Ahora tenemos otro grupo de estudiantes y no necesitamos las aulas de Google del año pasado. Y se sorprenderá de que no sea un proceso sencillo. Y hay una razón detrás de eso.

Entonces, ¿cómo eliminamos Google Classroom que ya no necesitamos? Vivir en un aula y en Google Classroom requiere dos pasos. Cuando abres Google Classroom, asegúrate de ir a clases y ver todas las clases. Quiero eliminar mi segundo Google Classroom. Enseñé a un grupo de estudiantes este año, y ahora no voy a enseñar en el año que viene y quiero eliminar esta clase. Ahora, si haces clic en tres puntos en la esquina superior derecha, no verás la opción de eliminar y aquí es donde la gente normalmente va a editar o eliminar, pero eliminar ya no está allí.

Debido a que Google Classroom está configurado de tal manera que antes de eliminarlo, debes archivarlo. Google

Classroom le advertirá que los alumnos no podrán acceder a esta clase, pero aparecerá en clases archivadas. Ahora, cuando se haya archivado, es cuando finalmente podemos eliminarlo. Haz clic en tres líneas en la esquina superior izquierda y desplácese hasta las clases archivadas. Verá la clase que se ha archivado. Ahora, cuando haz clic en tres puntos, verá una opción para eliminar. Y así es como borras tu clase de forma permanente.

Quizás te preguntes por qué necesito archivarlo primero y luego eliminarlo. Y esta es la respuesta. Cuando se archiva la clase, hay dos cosas que puedes hacer. Primero, siempre puedes restaurar esta clase. Si hago clic en Restaurar, se moverá hacia atrás y los estudiantes podrán acceder a él. Otra cosa que puedes hacer con las clases de archivo, puedes reutilizar las publicaciones realizadas en esta clase antes. Así que imaginemos que todavía enseño mi primera clase de Google y quiero reutilizar algunas publicaciones que se hicieron en mi segunda clase de Google y que la segunda clase de Google se ha archivado. No lo veo en mi pantalla de inicio, pero aún pude obtener o tomar algunos materiales de allí. Si voy al trabajo de clase en mi primera clase de Google, haz clic en Crear y luego en "reutilizar publicaciones". Notarás que en este selector de clases, todavía puedo ver mi segundo grupo Aula pequeña, aunque no la veo en mi pantalla de inicio, donde normalmente veo mis clases, puedo ver una vez que empiezo, usamos publicación, pero está marcado que ha sido archivado, puedo seleccionar mi segunda clase de Google y puedo usar algunas publicaciones que están allí. Y esa es la principal diferencia entre eliminar un archivo.

Entonces, en una nota final, hemos visto cómo mantener nuestro Google Classroom agradable y organizado. Veamos cómo podemos usar temas para compartimentar las publicaciones que hemos creado. Analizamos cómo podemos reutilizar publicaciones que se hicieron anteriormente. También miramos cómo archivar clases Cómo eliminar una clase, para que ya no sea visible ni en una pantalla de inicio ni en una clase archivada.

CONCLUSIÓN

Esta plataforma se presenta como una gran herramienta para incrementar la interacción en las clases, disminuir el consumo de papel y reducir los costos en escuelas y universidades.

Uno de los principales beneficios de esta plataforma es que se puede utilizar muy bien en *Blended learning*, que es una mezcla entre e-learning y aprendizaje convencional.

Recomiendo ampliamente esta herramienta para las instituciones educativas que estén pensando en migrar sus procesos a la vía digital (e-learning), usar esta plataforma en conjunto con clases presenciales (Aprendizaje Mixto), puede ayudarnos a hacer un progreso y migración amistosa.

En cuanto a la venta de cursos en Internet o la formación de personal, no tendrá ninguna posibilidad de utilizar esta infraestructura, ya que no ofrece ningún protocolo de seguridad de la información, lo que puede ser un problema en cuanto a la privacidad de los contenidos

Como puedes ver, en este libro he compartido contigo cómo lo uso, cómo creo las clases, invito a los alumnos, cómo asigno las tareas o cómo notificarlos en el tablero de la clase. Todo esto ahora nos hará estar más cerca que nunca de nuestros alumnos.

Espero que esta guía sobre cómo usar Google Classroom dentro y fuera del aula sea útil.

¡Buena suerte!

APRECIACIÓN

Agradecemos sinceramente tu compra de nuestro libro electrónico que revela información útil sobre todo lo que necesitas saber sobre Google Classroom. Esperamos que te guste.

Gracias

- *Anna Smith.*

CPSIA information can be obtained
at www.ICGtesting.com
Printed in the USA
LVHW051522130920
665874LV00011B/977

9 798676 640866